CORINTHIANS
1 and 2

Edwin Robertson has had a varied career since taking his first church in Luton. After the War he left his pastorate in St Albans and joined the Religious Affairs Branch of the Control Commission, British Zone of Germany, where he developed a deep understanding of German theological thinking, particularly the works of Dietrich Bonhoeffer, whose papers he has since edited in English.

After Germany he was Assistant Head of Religious Broadcasting at the B.B.C. for seven years, and then in 1956 became Study Secretary of the United Bible Societies, based in Geneva. His work was to undertake a study on 'The Place and Use of the Bible in the Living Situation of the Churches', and involved contact with a great number of churches throughout the world, getting information from them and helping them to use the Bible more effectively.

Mr Robertson is at present Associate Director of the World Association for Christian Communication, and also minister of Westbourne Park Baptist Church, London.

THE J. B. PHILLIPS' COMMENTARIES
edited by J. B. Phillips and E. H. Robertson

LUKE   John Drury
CORINTHIANS 1 AND 2   E. H. Robertson

To be published shortly

MATTHEW   John Marsh
MARK   J. B. Phillips
JOHN   John Riches

THE J. B. PHILLIPS' COMMENTARIES

CORINTHIANS
1 and 2

by

E. H. Robertson

Collins

FONTANA BOOKS

First published in Fontana Books, 1973
© E. H. Robertson 1973

Printed in Great Britain
Collins Clear-Type Press
London and Glasgow

To Westbourne Park Baptist Church

Translator's Preface

In 1941 when I began translating the Epistles of the New Testament I was vicar of a much-bombed parish in S.E. London. I wrote primarily because, rather to my surprise, I found that the young people in my youth club did not understand the English of the Authorized Version. For that matter neither did the bulk of my faithful church people, and many of them had long ago given up the attempt to understand the Epistles. They regarded them as obscure and difficult as well as having little bearing on the sort of lives we were then living.

My work therefore began with a double purpose: first to translate from the Greek into English that people would understand, and secondly to show that through the translation itself and by small study groups these first-century documents, quite often addressed to Christians in danger, had a peculiar relevance to us at that time.

I had few qualifications apart from a working knowledge of New Testament Greek and a good direct English vocabulary. Long before I had any idea of being a translator, I deliberately trained myself in what is nowadays called communication. Books were almost impossible to procure and my tools for the work of translation were meagre. Indeed, I was not even able to find an up-to-date Greek text until just after the war; and the spate of books about the words used and their particular meanings in the New Testament had not yet been published.

In spite of such handicaps and sheer shortage of time the original work of translation, even though it was not published in book form until 1947, proved what I had long suspected – that lay people know far less about what is actually written in the New Testament than they are ever likely to admit. I am not at all sure that the majority of trained clergy realize this is still true today. When I read week by week of the commentaries and books about the Faith which seem to pour out unendingly, I suspect that they can only reach a very small circle. Indeed, if I did nothing else I should only be able to read a very small proportion of them, which is in fact what I do. I do not for a moment say that such books should not be written, but I feel I must state my conviction that unless they are read, digested and reissued in simpler form, despite all the research and labour involved, the vast majority even of church-going people will be none the wiser.

Thus, in spite of the quite large number of commentaries on books of the New Testament which have appeared in recent years, it seems to me there is room for a commentary of rather a different nature with rather a different purpose. My publisher and various trusted friends agree that there is such a need. We aim simply to help people to lead a Christian life in this puzzling and anxiety-torn modern world. Thus, if we believe in the unique inspiration of the New Testament documents, the commentator is, so to speak, taking the reader by the hand and pointing out (a) the meaning and significance of each particular passage in its historic setting, and (b) what the passage means to the disciple of Christ today.

This means a certain amount of simplification and the sustained refusal to enter into scholastic controversies, however fascinating these may be to the expert in the New Testament field. I cannot believe that the average intelligent modern reader is much concerned about the continually changing battle-ground of ascribing authorship for this or that passage. He is not interested in 'proto-Luke', 'Ur-Mark', the mysterious and elusive 'Q' or the various 'Johns', though they may have to be briefly mentioned. But he is deeply interested in the historic reliability of what he reads and in what it means or could mean to him today.

We have therefore requested men who are sound in scholarship to write these commentaries, but who are concerned primarily with the pastoral value of the work they are to do. They will try to illuminate and instruct, to provoke thought as well as to awaken and strengthen faith.

J. B. PHILLIPS

Introduction

Paul's dealings with Corinth are described in the Acts of the Apostles and in the surviving letters that he wrote to the Christians at Corinth. His first contact seems to have been during what is called the second missionary journey. It was on that journey that he crossed over into Europe for the first time and at Philippi he met his first pagan opposition. The old pattern returned when he got to Thessalonica and Beroea: he began with the synagogues, persuaded some Jews and some Greek believers to become followers of Christ, then other Jews stirred up trouble with the civil authorities and Paul was eventually detained or chased out of town. He had left Philippi with honour, but he had to leave Thessalonica in a hurry. *Without delay the brothers despatched Paul and Silas off to Beroea that night.* (Acts 17.10) And he had also to leave Beroea in the same way. He came to Athens alone, intending to wait there for Silas and Timothy to join him. He used the opportunity to preach to the Greeks in Athens, but with no great success. With all this behind him and still very much worried about the young believers he had left behind in Thessalonica, he came to Corinth. He came in low spirits, having apparently almost given up his missionary work. He returned to his old trade and he might well have been forgotten, an obscure tent-maker in Corinth, if he had not been aroused from his depression by some fellow-Christians with whom he stayed. Looking back some years later on his arrival in Corinth, he could describe his state of mind fairly accurately. *As a matter of fact, in myself I was feeling far from strong; I was nervous and rather shaky.* (1 Corinthians 2.3)

After this inauspicious beginning, Paul stayed about eighteen months at Corinth and it was the scene of his greatest success so far.

CORINTH

Corinth had been of considerable importance in the days of the Greek city states. It was destroyed by the Romans and rebuilt by Julius Caesar as the capital of the Province of Achaia. Its importance was largely geographical. It lay on a narrow neck of land which attached the Peloponnese to the mainland. A few years after Paul arrived there, the Emperor Nero had a plan for digging a canal across this narrow neck of land. This canal was not completed until modern times and it considerably shortened the sea-route from the ports of the Aegean to those of the Adriatic. In Paul's time, with no canal, the goods were unloaded at one of the ports of Corinth, carried across the narrow neck of land, and loaded again on to other boats. This gave Corinth a busy and prosperous trade and, of course, with it a mixed population and the usual unsavoury reputation of a sea-port. Paul's companions found him in Corinth. They would have no difficulty because Christians nearly always grouped together in these ancient towns. It was usually in the Jewish quarter that the Christians settled. Paul himself, when he first went to Corinth, *found a Jew called Aquila, a native of Pontus. This man had recently come from Italy with his wife Priscilla, because Claudius had issued a decree that all Jews should leave Rome.* (Acts 18.1, 2) We are told that that decree of Claudius' was issued because of some riots in the Jewish quarter caused by a man called Chresto, obviously a garbled account of the word Christ. The pagans usually had a distorted image of Christians as a rather quarrelsome Jewish sect. Paul inevitably clashed with the orthodox Jews. He was hardly tactful in setting up his base next to a synagogue in a house belonging to gentile worshippers. *By the time Silas and Timothy arrived from Macedonia Paul was completely absorbed in preaching the message, showing the Jews as clearly as he could that Jesus is Christ.* (Acts 18.5) The usual pattern followed and the Jews made mischief with the civil authorities and tried to get him expelled. This time they failed, and the fact that the case was dismissed against him greatly strengthened his position. For the first time on his missionary journeys, he was able to settle down for a considerable period. During these eighteen months he built up a large and very active, if somewhat turbulent, community! It was predominantly gentile and was later to cause him a great deal of trouble. He left Corinth in the middle of A.D. 52 and made his way back to Jerusalem and Antioch. The account of that stay in Corinth can be read in the Acts of the Apostles, Chapter 18, verses 1–50.

WRITING TO THE CORINTHIANS

Paul began his third missionary journey a year later, and after a number of visits to other churches, he headed for Ephesus and settled down there for about two and a half years. He had learned the value of having a settled base at Corinth and he was to use that experience now in Ephesus. From Ephesus he was able to send out letters and receive answers. He was driven almost to distraction by the problems in his many churches, especially the church at Corinth. While at Ephesus he sent some of his staff to visit the church and once crossed the Aegean himself. Otherwise, his main contact with Corinth was by letter or by report.

In the New Testament we have two letters by Paul to the Christians at Corinth, but Paul wrote at least four letters. He referred to an earlier letter in 1 Corinthians: *In my previous letter I said, 'Don't mix with the immoral.'* (1 Corinthians 5.9) That letter is almost completely lost and we have no idea of its date. It was written while Paul was in Ephesus and probably near the beginning of his stay there. The only surviving part of the letter is embedded in what we call the second letter to the Christians at Corinth. 2 Corinthians 6.14–7.1 is almost certainly a part of that early lost letter.

Towards the end of A.D. 56, while Paul was still at Ephesus, a Christian delegation arrived to ask certain questions: *I am very glad that Stephanas, Fortunatus and Achaicus have arrived. They have made up for what you were unable to do. They have relieved my anxiety and yours. You should appreciate having men like that!* (1 Corinthians 16.17–18) He had already received news of the church at Corinth from Apollos and from the household of Chloe. This was mostly disturbing news about divisions in the church and had led him to write what we call 1 Corinthians. This letter seems to have been written a little before Easter A.D. 57.

After this, some crisis arose in Corinth and Paul was compelled to pay a short visit himself. He refers to this visit as a *painful visit.* (2 Corinthians 2.1) He promised that he would pay a longer visit later, but this never took place. Instead he sent a representative with full authority. The Corinthians were obviously angered that Paul did not come himself. A second crisis arose and they flouted his authority. Still Paul did not pay another visit, but instead sent a severe letter. This severe letter is preserved at the end of 2 Corinthians. It is 2 Corinthians 10–13. It apparently had the desired effect, but Paul was very anxious after he had sent it and waited with some uncertainty for its results. In fact, he had already left Ephesus before he knew that it had been well received: *Well, when I came to Troas to preach the gospel of Christ, although there was an obvious God-given opportunity, I must confess I was on edge the whole time because there was no sign of brother Titus. So I said good-bye and went from there to Macedonia.* (2 Corinthians 2.12–13) It was in Macedonia that he heard the good news from Titus that all was well.

He then wrote his fourth letter, which is the greater part of 2 Corinthians, in fact, chapters 1–9.

So we can see in these four letters the developing relationship of Paul with the church at Corinth. The value of the letters lies in showing us the way in which the apostle dealt with the young church in the midst of all its temptations and difficulties. Almost incidentally he deals with issues that have remained important issues for the Christian church ever since.

The First Letter
to the Christians at Corinth

Chapter 1

Vs 1-3 Paul, commissioned by the will of God as a messenger of Christ Jesus, and Sosthenes, a Christian brother, to the Church of God at Corinth – to those whom Christ Jesus has made holy, who are called to be God's men and women, to all true believers in Jesus Christ, their Lord and ours – grace and peace be to you from God the Father and the Lord, Jesus Christ!

In writing this letter to Corinth, Paul associates Sosthenes with him. They could hardly fail to remember him in Corinth. After Paul had been cleared by the magistrate and the Jews could do nothing to harm him, they were angry and *seized . . . the president of the synagogue* who had been friendly to Paul and *beat him in front of the court-house*. That was Sosthenes. We read that the magistrate, *Gallio remained completely unconcerned*. (Acts 18.12–17) Sosthenes must have come with the delegation from Corinth to ask Paul some questions of procedure at Corinth and he remained some time in Ephesus with Paul. By mentioning his name here Paul is assuring the Corinthians that he is well informed about what is going on in Corinth!

He gives his usual greetings and seems to underline those characteristics of a Christian community which appear to be weak in Corinth. He adds to his usual greetings, as a kind of parenthesis: *to those whom Christ has made holy, who are called to be God's men and women, to all true believers in Jesus Christ, their Lord and ours.* Like some overture to an opera which contains a foretaste of many of the melodies later to come, these few verses tell us already that Paul is going to deal with being *holy*, being *God's men*, being *true* believers and the *unity* of faith.

Vs 4–9 I am always thankful to God for what the gift of his grace in Christ Jesus has meant to you. For, as the Christian message has become established among you, he has enriched your whole lives, from the words on your lips to the understanding in your hearts. And you have been eager to receive his gifts during this time of waiting for his final appearance. He will keep you steadfast in the faith to the end, so that when his day comes you need fear no condemnation. God is utterly dependable, and it is he who has called you into fellowship with his Son Jesus Christ, our Lord.

He continues to keep them waiting for the main purpose of the letter. He expresses his thanks for their faith and for what the gift of grace *has meant to you*. There is no doubt about the growth of the church at Corinth. As this faith has spread, what has it done? Paul begins by saying what it should have done and he expresses this as though he assumes it has really happened, although from all that he has heard from Sosthenes and the household of Chloe, the real situation in Corinth is far from what he describes here. Such grace surely has *enriched your whole lives*, and this in two special areas – *your lips* and the *understanding in your hearts*. He knows what they have been saying and he also knows that they boast of being rather superior people, understanding great mysteries. He presses further. They have been *eager to receive* the gifts of the Spirit. He will soon be exposing their false eagerness to receive only the showy gifts of the Spirit like speaking with tongues. In the next few verses he uses words that echo his concern, although his tone is still that of praise: *steadfast in the faith, fear no condemnation, God is utterly dependable, called . . . into fellowship*. While his readers must have been pleased at the praise, they would have an uneasy feeling as they heard these particular phrases, because they were not steadfast, they were ready to condemn, they were not dependable, and their fellowship was shattered.

Vs 10-12 Now I do beg you, my brothers, by all that our Lord Jesus Christ means to you, to speak with one voice, and not allow yourselves to be split up into parties. All together you should be achieving a unity in thought and judgment. For I know, from what some of Chloe's people have told me, that you are each making different claims – 'I am one of Paul's men,' says one; 'I am one of Apollos',' says another; or 'I am one of Cephas' '; while someone else says, 'I owe my faith to Christ alone.'

Paul's first qualification of his praise is to refer to their divisions. He appeals to them to *speak with one voice* and not to divide up into parties. They should be one in thought and judgment, but *Chloe's people* have given him disturbing news and probably Sosthenes also. The divisions take the form of supporting one type of preacher. Even Paul's name is used as a party cry. Apollos is preferred by others because he appears to be the kind of eloquent preacher who attracts crowds. In this letter there are many references to show that Paul had Apollos often in mind. He describes true preaching as not depending upon eloquence or upon cleverness, but upon the power of God. But at this point he is not criticizing Apollos, only their use of his name as a party cry. The same applies to Cephas, i.e. Peter, who is used as a symbol of the original church, the true church, before this upstart Paul began to put his own interpretation upon it. Even those who were probably nearest to Paul, who maintain that they *owe their faith to Christ alone*, are condemned for making a party issue out of it. There is absolute clarity in Paul's attack, and if it was particularly necessary at Corinth in his day, it has

continued to be necessary for every church in every age.
There are those who follow men, those who pride themselves on purity of doctrine, and those who dismiss all new
ideas. There are parties, much as there are denominations,
and this letter opens with a direct attack upon all parties
and divisions.

Vs 13–18 What *are* you saying? Is there more than one
Christ? Was it Paul who died on the cross for you? Were
you baptized in the name of Paul? It makes me thankful
that I didn't actually baptize any of you (except Crispus
and Gaius), or perhaps someone would be saying I did it in
my own name. (Oh yes, I did baptize Stephanas' family,
but I can't remember anyone else.) For Christ did not
send me primarily to baptize, but to proclaim the gospel.
And I have not done this by the persuasiveness of clever
words, for I have no desire to rob the cross of its power.
The preaching of the cross is, I know, nonsense to those
who are involved in this dying world, but to us who are
being saved from that death it is nothing less than the
power of God.

Having exposed the divisions and assured the Corinthians
that he knows about them and disapproves of all their parties,
Paul goes into the reasons why these divisions are a serious
hindrance to the church. They imply that there is *more than
one Christ* or that the leaders they so much admire are to be
compared with him. 'Let us get this quite clear,' he says,
'there is one Christ who died for you, into whose name you
are baptized, etc.' The mention of baptism leads to an important digression. Any convert is liable to become specially
attached to the man who baptizes him. Perhaps this is why
Jesus did not baptize, but only his disciples. Paul sees the
danger and spontaneously expresses his thanks that he did
not baptize any of them. Then he remembers that there were

a few, but not enough to make a party. He may suspect that Apollos had baptized some when he was there and that they are forming the Apollos party around his converts. Apollos appears to have been an interesting character. Paul tries not to be jealous of him, but he doesn't quite succeed!

We meet Apollos in Acts 18.24–28, where he is said to be a powerful preacher, *a Jew . . . of Alexandria*. He arrived in Ephesus already a convert, but not yet fully instructed. Aquila and Priscilla, who had given hospitality to Paul when he first arrived in Corinth, appear to have been wanderers. They came from Rome to Corinth and we find them in Ephesus when Apollos arrives. They were devout souls who *explained the Way of God to him more accurately*, i.e. to Apollos. He then crossed over to Corinth and probably just missed Paul who had left for Ephesus. But Paul heard plenty about this gifted preacher and now one of the sects is a party saying, *I am one of Apollos'*. There are indications throughout the letter that Paul is disturbed by this party because they attach too much importance to eloquence and cleverness. Apparently there was a kind of intellectual élite in the church of Corinth. Paul, after saying that he did not come *primarily to baptize*, has a slight dig at this party with his assurance that he did not proclaim the gospel *by the persuasiveness of clever words*. The danger is that the cleverness of the preacher may lead to admiration of him rather than acceptance of the power of the scandal of the cross. Paul had learnt this lesson with his ineffectual preaching in Athens. After that experience, which led to his fit of depression in Corinth and almost to his leaving the ministry, he began to see the power of the cross as the only power in Christian preaching. Talk of a crucified Christ appears to be nonsense to those who think a Saviour must always be a victor. A powerful contrast comes to the apostle's mind which has meaning still. Those *involved in this dying world* can only judge by the standards of the

Roman Empire. There, an emperor who is assassinated is a failure. Paul is writing at a time when this is no remote possibility. Strong emperors like Augustus did not get assassinated, weak emperors did. But Christians are not *involved in this dying world*. They are being saved and their secret is that the apparent defeat of the cross is *nothing less than the power of God*. This leads to a discussion on the nature of true wisdom which, while not directed against Apollos, is directed against those who see in his brilliance the real power of preaching. There are two wisdoms – God's wisdom and man's wisdom. They are not the same.

Vs 19–25   It is written:
    I will destroy the wisdom of the wise,
    And the prudence of the prudent will I reject.
For consider, what have the philosopher, the writer and the critic of this world to show for all their wisdom? Has not God made the wisdom of this world look foolish? For it was after the world in its wisdom had failed to know God, that he in his wisdom chose to save all who would believe by the 'simple-mindedness' of the gospel message. For the Jews ask for miraculous proofs and the Greeks an intellectual panacea, but all we preach is Christ crucified – a stumbling-block to the Jews and sheer nonsense to the gentiles, but for those who are called, whether Jews or Greeks, Christ the power of God and the wisdom of God. And this is really only natural, for God's 'foolishness' is wiser than men, and his 'weakness' is stronger than men.

When Isaiah encouraged the depressed people of God long ago with an assurance that God would deliver Jerusalem, he did not say that the Jews were clever enough to resist the Assyrians or outwit them. He said that God would *destroy* their *wisdom* and *reject* their prudence. Paul is quoting loosely from Isaiah 29.14. This has remained true. *What have the philosopher, the writer and the critic of this world to show for all their wisdom?* Paul implies that they have very little to show. God has accomplished more things through simple integrity than he has through the cleverness of men. Paul is still trying to convince the Corinthians that there are more important gifts than so-called wisdom. He had been to Athens, the very centre of culture in the ancient world, and still a symbol of it. There he had seen that the wisest men the world had ever known had been unable to recognize God. All their wisdom had been foolishness beside the *simple-mindedness* of the gospel. A man is not saved by a first-class degree or by an ability to discern or learn a language or even to reach the moon. He is saved by quite simply accepting *the gospel message* and living by it. Paul uses the examples of his day. The Jews need a miraculous sign to assure them that God is present. They need Gideon's fleece again or a sign such as they asked from Jesus and he would not give. The Greeks, on the other hand, have to be convinced by answers to all their questions, *an intellectual panacea*. The gospel message is not of miracles nor of persuasive arguments, it is quite simply, *Christ crucified*. A Saviour who was put to death! Such a message would be a scandal to any Jew who had a clear idea as to what was expected of the Christ or Messiah. The Greek word does in fact mean just *stumbling-block*, but from the sound of that Greek word we have derived a new word, *scandal*, which is precisely what this message was to any devout Jew – scandalous, blasphemous – and it nearly always made him very angry, as Paul's experiences with the Jews bear witness. But what of those who have no idea of a Christ? They do have ideas of a saviour – all the popular cults and religions of the day offered ways of salvation – and to them this message was *sheer foolishness*. How could he who was unable to save himself save his followers? And experience showed that these followers were not spared much. They were often despised and poor, drawn largely from the slave class. So whichever way you look, the wisdom of this world did not think much of the gospel message. It was no more acceptable to Jews than it was to gentiles. But there were some, and they included Jews and gentiles, who believed the message. These are described as *those who are called*, because it is so incredible that anyone could accept the message on his own initiative. Paul thought of them as being called by God. These can see that there is both *power* and *wisdom* in the simple gospel message. The power is shown by their new ability to cope with life and to face death unafraid; the wisdom is shown by the new understanding they have of the world. Paul again echoes the prophets in his explanation of this paradox. In many ways the prophets had talked of God's ways being different from man's ways, higher than man's. So now, even *God's 'foolishness'* – a worldly judgment on what he has done in Christ – proves to be *wiser than* the greatest wisdom of men; and *his 'weakness'* – a typical judgment on his allowing Christ to be crucified – proves to be *stronger than* the greatest power of man. Nor are God's values the same as man's.

Vs 26–31 For look at your own calling as Christians, my brothers. You don't see among you many of the wise (according to this world's judgment) nor many of the ruling class, nor many from the noblest families. But God has chosen what the world calls foolish to shame the wise; he has chosen what the world calls weak to shame the strong. He has chosen things of little strength and small repute, yes and even things which have no real existence, to explode the pretensions of the things that are – that no man may boast in the presence of God. Yet from this same God you have received your standing in Jesus Christ, and he has become for us the true wisdom, a matter, in practice, of being made righteous and holy, in fact, of being redeemed. And this makes us see the truth of the scripture: He that glorieth, let him glory in the Lord.

Like the ancient people of God in the Old Testament, Christians are not to regard themselves as superior to others. The whole idea of Christians as an *élite* is foreign to the simple gospel message. Paul is brutally frank. The Corinthians really had very little to feel superior about. The preaching of the gospel had not attracted the most brilliant nor the best people. This wisdom they talk about is not well illustrated in the church members! Their members are not drawn from *the ruling class* nor from *the noblest families*. The glory of the church has always been that God took *what the world calls* ordinary people and made them extraordinary. The glory is all of God, all is given. God did not choose the 'best'. *He has chosen things of little strength and small repute.* As Paul goes on to extend this he elaborates the same theme. The conclusion is simple. If you want to boast, boast at the wonder of God's grace, that he could do this *even* with you! *Glory in the Lord,* not yourself.

Vs 1–5 In the same way, my brothers, when I came to proclaim to you God's secret purpose, I did not come equipped with any brilliance of speech or intellect. You may as well know now that it was my secret determination to concentrate entirely on Jesus Christ himself and the fact of his death upon the cross. As a matter of fact, in myself I was feeling far from strong; I was nervous and rather shaky. What I said and preached had none of the attractiveness of the clever mind, but it was a demonstration of the power of the Spirit! Plainly God's purpose was that your faith should rest not upon man's cleverness but upon the power of God.

Paul is unable to get away from the thought that the preference for Apollos was for all the wrong reasons. We can deduce that he was a gifted preacher, but they were putting far too much importance on *brilliance of speech or intellect*. Paul had no such gift when he came to *proclaim . . . God's secret purpose*. Here he uses a word which was in itself an implied criticism. He knew that they were still toying with pagan religions, particularly those strange mystery religions which were sweeping Asia Minor at the same time. These revivals of old religions offered salvation to those who understood the mysteries and were initiated in them. Some Corinthians saw Christianity as a kind of mystery religion. Apollos fitted the role of a mystery preacher. He was brilliant and he was intellectual. Paul could be that at times too, but on the serious occasions of preaching the gospel he had to show the difference. God had his mysteries, his secret purposes, but these were totally different from the mysteries of the pagans. In fact, Paul had learnt his lesson at Athens before he came to Corinth and he had made a promise to himself, a *secret determination*, to keep off all cleverness and *concentrate entirely on Jesus Christ*. The Corinthians might retort that he was their great Saviour and his mysteries were their special knowledge. Paul anticipates this retort. He adds – *and the fact of his death upon the cross*. He meant the down-to-earth fact of a criminal's death, not a jewelled cross, not 'crucified between two candles on the altar, but between two thieves on a tree'. Away with all prettiness or fancy magic! Away with brilliance and intellect! He is not attacking Apollos, but he is denouncing the false ideas of God's mysteries or of real preaching. If they will think back, the gospel which converted them was not a brilliant piece of oratory by a splendid preacher. Paul was ill, weak, nervous and shaky. What he preached *had none of the attractiveness of the clever mind*. But what did it do? It saved Corinth and a church was born. *It was a demonstration of the power of the Spirit!* The danger lingers in the church. Brilliant preaching is still attractive and we still need showing that our *faith rests upon the power of God* and *not upon man's cleverness*. Sometimes, as in Corinth, God will make his preachers sound feeble in order that the glory may be his and not be accounted the result of clever preaching or brilliant argument. The failure of many an evangelistic campaign is that the preacher was too good. The Corinthians wanted something special, they were given something quite ordinary. In that ordinary message by a poor preacher was hidden the *power of God*. Let that suffice!

Vs 6–12 We do, of course, speak 'wisdom' among those who are spiritually mature, but it is not what is called wisdom by this world, nor by the powers-that-be, who soon will be only the powers that have been. The wisdom we speak of is that mysterious secret wisdom of God which he planned before the creation for our glory today. None of the powers of this world have known this wisdom – if they had they would never have crucified the Lord of glory! But, as it is written:

> Things which eye saw not, and ear heard not,
> And which entered not into the heart of man,
> Whatsoever things God prepared for them that love him.

Thus God has, through the Spirit, let us share his secret. For nothing is hidden from the Spirit, not even the deep wisdom of God. For who could really understand a man's inmost thoughts except the spirit of the man himself? How much less could anyone understand the thoughts of God except the very Spirit of God? We have now received not the spirit of the world but the Spirit of God himself, so that we can understand something of God's generosity towards us.

Paul was not going to let Apollos get away with it all! He has made his point that *the power of God* is the true source of their salvation. But Paul too could proclaim mysteries, he too could *speak 'wisdom'*. However, he reserved this for those who had the maturity to understand, only *among those who are spiritually mature*. Three times in the few lines of the last section he used the word *wisdom*, and always to disapprove! He contrasts the *wisdom* they admire with proclaiming *God's secret purposes* or *the fact* of Christ's *death upon the cross* or the weakness of the preacher or the true *demonstration of the power of the Spirit* or simply *the power of God*. Now he begins this section with that same word. He deliberately places it first in the Greek – 'wisdom we speak', but he goes on to say what he means by true wisdom. *It is not what is called wisdom by this world,* nor, he implies, the kind of wisdom these Corinthian Christians appear to seek! As Paul defines this true wisdom he uses again that word *mystery* – that *mysterious secret wisdom of God*. What Paul means by wisdom is nothing less than the whole divine plan of creation, salvation and restoration of all things in the final purpose of God. His most complete treatment of this is in Romans 8 where the whole chapter deals with the secret wisdom of God, including the verse: 'The whole creation is on tiptoe to see the wonderful sight of the sons of God coming into their own.' (Romans 8.19) With this grand conception you can see why Paul was so angry with their petty ideas about wisdom. He repeats the word until they must have been heartily sorry that they ever mentioned it! God's secret wisdom was planned before the creation of the world and it is his plan for us. The world does not know it or understand it, but the simplest Christian has it deep in his heart. He may not be able to define it or use the proper theological terms, but he knows it and it is this consciousness, that God has prepared such things for his children, that gives to the Christian an inner peace and confidence. The outstanding example of the blindness of this world to God's secret wisdom is the stupid act of *the powers of this world* crucifying *the Lord of glory*! They would hardly have done this if they had known that he was *the Lord of glory*! But the church has a foretaste of that glory and understands where the wisest of this world do not. Paul quotes freely from his favourite book, and he wasn't worried much about First, Second and Third Isaiah! To him the Book of Isaiah contained truth about God and his people. He quotes very freely, paraphrasing rather than translating, Isaiah 64.4. Many have been blind to God's secret wisdom, but *God has, through the Spirit, let us share his secret*. This is how Paul interprets Isaiah's words about the *things God prepared for them that love him*. The communicator here is the Spirit. Paul explains by analogy. It is only the spirit of man that can explain *man's inmost thoughts*. You cannot get inside a man's thought by an external study of man, by weighing him or measuring him! So with God. The only way to understand the secret wisdom of God is by the Spirit of God. *Nothing is hidden from the Spirit, not even the deep wisdom of God.* Paul is on the edge of developing a doctrine of the Spirit here which is of countless value to succeeding generations of Christians. We can only understand the wisdom which Paul talks about if we have received *the Spirit of God himself*, and such wisdom beggars the wisdom of this world by comparison.

Vs 13–16 It is these things that we talk about, not using the expressions of the human intellect but those which the Holy Spirit teaches us, explaining spiritual things to those who are spiritual.

But the unspiritual man simply cannot accept the matters which the Spirit deals with – they just don't make sense to him, for, after all, you must be spiritual to see spiritual things. The spiritual man, on the other hand, has an insight into the meaning of everything, though his insight may baffle the man of the world. This is because the former is sharing in God's wisdom, and

Who hath known the mind of the Lord,

That he should instruct him?

Nevertheless, we who are spiritual have the very thoughts of Christ!

Chapter 3

Vs 1–8 I, my brothers, was unable to talk to you as spiritual men: I had to talk to you as unspiritual, as yet babies in the Christian life. And my practice has been to feed you, as it were, with 'milk' and not with 'meat'. You were unable to digest 'meat' in those days and I don't believe you can do it now. For you are still unspiritual; all the time that there is jealousy and squabbling among you you show that you are – you are living just like men of the world. While one of you says, 'I am one of Paul's converts' and another says, 'I am one of Apollos'', are you not plainly unspiritual?

After all, who is Apollos? Who is Paul? No more than servants through whom you came to believe as the Lord gave each man his opportunity. I may have done the planting and Apollos the watering, but it was God who made the seed grow! The planter and the waterer are nothing compared with him who gives life to the seed. Planter and waterer are alike insignificant, though each shall be rewarded according to his particular work.

The division between *spiritual* and *unspiritual* is not only between Christians and non-Christians. The line runs through the church itself. Corinth had prided itself on being sophisticated. They were flattered by the preaching of Apollos and considered that Paul did not understand their intellectual standards. They were not like his barbarians of Galatia! They wanted difficult sermons. Here Paul's doctrine of the Spirit comes out more clearly. He would have preached more developed and more spiritual sermons if they had been ready for them. You can't talk about the subtleties of language to a man who has not yet learnt to read or even speak the language properly. Some do, of course, but they are not communicating. The analogy of food is the most natural. Milk for babies and meat for grown-up men. The Corinthians are babes in spiritual things. One of their complaints was obviously that he had not treated them as adults when he was first in Corinth. Why did he not explain the intricacies of Christian theology, as Apollos had? The reason is that they were not ready for this advanced stuff. 'And,' says Paul, 'if we are to judge from your behaviour, you're not ready yet.' Maturity is not just a matter of intellectual ability. What they are talking about is a spiritual quality, and this shows itself in their behaviour. *For you are still unspiritual; all the time that there is jealousy and squabbling among you you show that you are – you are living just like men of the world*, and by that Paul means *unspiritual*. If there is a division to be drawn between spiritual and unspiritual, that line runs through Corinth, or perhaps Corinth is already on the wrong side of the line! The evidence is their party splits, running after preachers or leaders. But who are these preachers – Apollos, Paul, Peter? Here he uses two analogies: one from gardening, one from architecture. In gardening, the apostles and preachers are simply the gardeners – watering, hoeing, tending. Who actually causes the growth? Not them! In architecture, the apostles are simply the bricks or arches, parts of the building. Who provides the foundation without which the whole building falls down? Not them! God has provided a foundation and he makes the seed grow.

Vs 9–15 In this work, we work with God, and that means that you are a field under God's cultivation, or, if you like, a house being built to his plan. I, like a master-builder who knows his job, by the grace God has given me, lay the foundation; someone else builds upon it. I only say this, let the builder be careful how he builds! The foundation is laid already, and no one can lay another, for it is Jesus Christ himself. But any man who builds on the foundation using as his material gold, silver, precious stones, wood, hay or straw, must know that each man's work will one day be shown for what it is. The day will show it plainly enough, for the day will arise in a blaze of fire, and that fire will prove the value of each man's work. If the work which a man has built upon the foundation stands this test, he will be rewarded. But if his work is burnt down, he loses it all. He personally will be safe, though rather like a man rescued from a fire.

Paul passes gladly from the analogy of gardening to that of architecture. All the preachers and the leaders in the church – Paul, Apollos, Peter, and any others – are *workers with God*. Corinth is not being cultivated by Paul or Apollos. *You are a field under God's cultivation, or, if you like, a house being built to his plan.* There are many kinds of workers still and it is not for us to say who is good and who is bad. Their work will be tested. Some will see their work destroyed, others will see it survive the test. There will be reward for work well done, but even those who build badly will not be destroyed by the test. Men may be sincerely wrong in what they are doing and they will grieve to discover how they have laboured in vain. But the church of Jesus Christ does not depend for its future upon the excellence of any man's work. The Corinthian Christians have too high an opinion of their intellectual capacity and too low an opinion of their spiritual heritage as Christians. They are not the followers of a school, but the cultivation of God. Paul has thus to lower their pride and raise their vision. They are to be nothing less than God's holy building.

Vs 16–23 Don't you realize that you yourselves are the temple of God, and that God's Spirit lives in you? God will destroy anyone who defiles his temple, for his temple is holy – *and that is exactly what you are!*

Let no one be under any illusion over this. If any man among you thinks himself one of the world's clever ones, let him discard his cleverness that he may learn to be truly wise. For this world's cleverness is stupidity to God. It is written:

> He that taketh the wise in their craftiness.

And again:

> The Lord knoweth the reasonings of the wise, that they are vain.

So let no one boast of men. Everything belongs to you! Paul, Apollos or Cephas; the world, life, death, the present or the future, everything is yours! For you belong to Christ, and Christ belongs to God!

After the analogy of gardening and architecture, Paul moves to the building of a temple. Their background is pagan and they are at home in such analogies. Temples are as common to them as churches to us. They live among people who look upon the desecration of a temple as something dreadful. A temple is holy because a god lives in it, and that god is thought of as bringing punishment to any who defile his temple. The Corinthians must learn that as Christians they are temples in which God's Spirit dwells. They must beware defiling such a temple. They cannot do what they please with their bodies, because God's *temple is holy* – and, he adds, *that is exactly what you are*.

Now Paul is ready to make the contrast between what the world calls *clever* and true wisdom. This is constantly a theme of the apostle's. He uses all the resources of the Old Testament to show that *this world's cleverness* when compared with the wisdom of God is stupid. The only wisdom worth boasting of is the wisdom of God, and that comes not from intellectual superiority but from the Spirit. He bids the Corinthians and us to stop priding ourselves upon an intellectual wisdom which is really rather stupid. Instead, remember that all things belong to a Christian – *Paul, Apollos or Cephas; the world, life, death, the present or the future, everything is yours!* The reason is not some intellectual achievement, but simply because *you belong to Christ*. Here is something worth boasting about, but of course it is not your own achievement, it is the free gift of God. Anyone can have it. There is no exclusiveness here which makes you feel superior to your fellowmen. Your pride is that *God's Spirit lives in you.*

Chapter 4

Vs 1–5 You should look upon us as ministers of Christ, as trustees of the secrets of God. And it is a prime requisite in a trustee that he should prove worthy of his trust. But, as a matter of fact, it matters very little to me what you, or any man, thinks of me – I don't even value my opinion of myself. For I might be quite ignorant of any fault in myself – but that doesn't justify me before God. My only true judge is the Lord.

The moral of this is that we should make no hasty or premature judgments. When the Lord comes he will bring into the light of day all that at present is hidden in darkness, and he will expose the secret motives of men's hearts. Then shall God himself give each man his share of praise.

What then is to be the role of the *ministers of Christ*? Never for a moment does Paul deny the validity of the others. He is distressed only that they are receiving attention as originators of the faith. He deplores such veneration to himself as much as to others. These men, Paul, Apollos, Cephas, are only servants. Their role is not that of originators, but of trustees, for which the *prime requisite* is to *prove worthy of trust*. That is all, not to impart some hidden new wisdom. Obviously there has been some direct criticism of Paul – he is not as good a speaker as Apollos, or he is not an original disciple like Peter, or he treats them like children, or some such thing. He disclaims any real concern for his own reputation: *it matters very little to me what you, or any man, thinks of me*. Only God can judge, and the Corinthians do ill to usurp the role of God.

Vs 6–7 I have used myself and Apollos above as an illustration, so that you might learn from what I have said about us not to assess man above his value in God's sight, and may thus avoid the pride which comes from making one teacher more important than another. For who makes you different from anybody else, and what have you got that was not given to you? And if anything has been given to you, why boast of it as if you had achieved it yourself?

There are other teachers in Corinth who claim to have special gifts. There always are! Men who claim that God has imparted some special knowledge to them or that they have discovered something new. The Corinthians have their share of this kind of spiritual pride. Paul attacks them directly. Perhaps they have some special gift, but what is that to boast of? They have nothing which was not given to them. Why then boast of what is given *as if you had achieved it yourself*? Now Paul turns to a little irony:

Vs 8–13 Oh, I know you are rich and flourishing! You've been living like kings, haven't you, while we've been away? I would to God you were really kings in God's sight so that we might reign with you!

I sometimes think that God means us, the messengers, to appear last in the procession of mankind, like the men who are to die in the arena. For indeed we are made a public spectacle before the angels of Heaven and the eyes of men. We are looked upon as fools, for Christ's sake, but you are wise in the Christian faith. We are considered weak, but you have become strong: you have found honour, we little but contempt. Up to this very hour we are hungry and thirsty, ill-clad, knocked about and practically homeless. We still have to work for our living by manual labour. Men curse us, but we return a blessing: they make our lives miserable but we take it patiently. They ruin our reputations but we go on trying to win them for God. We are the world's rubbish, the scum of the earth, yes, up to this very day.

The passage is full of images. The riches of kings belong to the self-styled leaders of Corinth, and Paul pretends to wish that he could share their prosperity. The contrast is pressed home, not so much to make the Corinthians ashamed as to show the true example of a Christian disciple of Christ. Many times Jesus had warned his followers to beware if they were prosperous or well thought of. The triumphal procession which the Corinthians knew well told only that one army was more powerful than the other. It never showed who was right. The leaders of Corinth are at the head of the procession while the apostles are captive chiefs at the end of it. The leaders of Corinth are said to be wise, but the apostles are called *fools*. Yet if we read the signs of the times clearly, it is the prisoners, the fools, who are Christ's. The contrast is painful, but Paul uses it to show that his wretched condition enables him to learn something about discipleship which they cannot learn with their prosperity. He can learn how to return a blessing for a curse, to be patient under persecution, to love and try to win those who ruin his reputation. It is after all worth being *the world's rubbish, the scum of the earth*. It is the best way to get close to Christ.

Vs 14–21 I don't write these things merely to make you feel uncomfortable, but that you may realize facts, as my dear children. After all, you may have ten thousand teachers in the Christian faith, but you cannot have many fathers! For in Christ Jesus I am your spiritual father through the gospel; that is why I implore you to follow the footsteps of me your father. I have sent Timothy to you to help you in this. For he himself is my much-loved and faithful son in the Lord, and he will remind you of those ways of living in Christ which I teach in every church to which I go.

Some of you have apparently grown conceited since I did not visit you. But please God it will not be long before I do come to you in person. Then I shall be able to see what power, apart from their words, these pretentious ones among you really possess. For the kingdom of God is not a matter of a spate of words but of the power of Christian living.

Now it's up to you to choose! Shall I come to you ready to chastize you, or in love and gentleness?

Paul claims a special authority, not as a superior teacher, but as a father. Even if they do prefer certain other preachers, no one can challenge his special position as the man who brought the gospel to them. As such, he claims to know how they should behave and what they should believe. He claims the authority of a father in those days – the Roman 'paterfamilias' or the Indian 'guru'. It is difficult to find an equivalent in modern western ways of life. It is not that Paul really claims to know any better or to be any wiser than others, but there is a special relationship with a man who in the name of Christ called them from darkness into light. He reinforces this by sending Timothy to them. This is both an assertion of authority and a cause of complaint. He can trust Timothy and he assumes the right to appoint their teacher. He does not come himself and that leads to complaints that he is a paper apostle, one who dare not rebuke them to their face. Rather like the man who is brave on the telephone! Timothy is to come, presumably with this letter, to show them what Paul is doing in the other churches and what he therefore expects from them. Paul also answers those who say that there is nothing to fear from an absentee apostle. *Some of you have apparently grown conceited since I did not visit you.* He threatens those who make this assumption with the promise that he will come. This promise is made somewhat rashly and he later regrets it. For the moment it is a good line. The boasters would be silenced by his avenging presence. They can have it any way they please. Let them choose the kind of Paul who will come. *Shall I come to you ready to chastize you, or in love and gentleness?* He can assume some guilty consciences as he begins to deal with specific points. He wants them to know that he is well informed about Corinth.

Chapter 5

Vs 1–8 It is actually reported that there is sexual immorality among you, and immorality of a kind that even pagans condemn – a man has apparently taken his father's wife! Are you still proud of yourselves? Shouldn't you be overwhelmed with sorrow? The man who has done such a thing should certainly be expelled from your fellowship!

I know I am not with you physically but I am with you in spirit, and I assure you as though I were actually with you that I have already pronounced judgment in the name of the Lord Jesus on the man who has done this thing. As one present in spirit when you are assembled, I say by the power of the Lord Jesus that the man should be left to the mercy of Satan so that while his body will experience the destructive powers of sin his spirit may yet be saved in the day of the Lord.

Your pride in yourselves is lamentably out of place. Don't you know how a little yeast can permeate the whole lump? Clear out every bit of the old yeast that you may be new unleavened bread! We Christians have had a Passover lamb sacrificed for us – none other than Christ himself! So let us 'keep the feast' with no trace of the yeast of the old life, nor the yeast of vice and wickedness, but with the unleavened bread of unadulterated truth!

Paul comes now to specific points. No doubt the reader has been waiting for this moment. What was the apostle driving at? It was not like him to spend so much time on their disregard of him. He had something which had to be said. Here it was – some particularly bad form of immorality which *even pagans condemn*. That was something in Corinth because it was known as a permissive city. Incest was condemned even by pagans, although here it probably refers to a stepmother. The Corinthians obviously believe or half-believe that being Christians they are above the law. We now begin to see the seriousness of Paul's reference to them as thinking themselves superior. He now treats them as children indeed. *Are you still proud of yourselves?* This revelation that he knew all about the incestuous man was calculated to shock them. They had read of his condemnation of their divisions and would perhaps put on a show of remorse for this, but the tolerance of a man who had behaved in such a way that pagans could point a finger at the Christian community obviously was intended to be hidden from the apostle. He speaks firmly now without argument: *The man . . . should certainly be expelled from your fellowship!* Paul was unforgiving. He was perhaps a little frightened of the effect of his own teaching. This is what the Judaisers, those old enemies of Paul who had insisted upon the Mosaic law, said would happen. Once you talk of freedom you soon find lesser people interpreting liberty as licence. He asserts his full authority, equally valid whether he is present or not. The punishment is harsh, *the man should be left to the mercy of Satan.* This is solemn excommunication, which it was assumed would lead to sickness and death. Then comes a strange mercy – the mercy of Satan indeed! *So that while his body will experience the destructive powers of sin his spirit may yet be saved in the day of the Lord.* A strange teaching for our day, but we must not confuse it with its later perversion. Paul was not handing this man over to a civil power to punish him. He was leaving him to the *mercy of Satan.* He hoped that in this way the man might be punished, but his spirit would not be destroyed. If he were allowed to remain in the church, tolerated in the name of freedom, he would not only pervert the church, but would endanger his own salvation. The church of Paul's day lived constantly under the awareness of Christ's return. If he were to return to Corinth, the man would be in danger of condemnation. It is, therefore, also for his own sake that Paul says, and brooks no argument now, that *the man who has done such a thing should certainly be expelled from your fellowship! . . . left to the mercy of Satan, that his spirit may yet be saved.* Punishment is never for destruction only, but also for purging. The church must be purged because *a little yeast can permeate the whole lump.* The example of yeast is always used in the Bible in a bad sense, except when Jesus uses the example of the yeast growing in the dough for the church changing the world. Here the more usual bad sense is meant. If the man remains, all discipline in the church will be undermined. Then the Corinthians would have a church of which they could not be proud. As it is, Paul sees dangers that they are proud of themselves for being liberal enough to tolerate anything. Such pride is, as he says, *out of place.* He calls for purity. At this point the rabbi in him comes out very clearly. The Passover, which has been applied to the death of Christ as the Paschal lamb, serves as his text. There, unleavened bread is used, not the leavened bread with *the yeast of vice and wickedness.* The Corinthians are seen as men who had come from paganism, with all the impurity which is symbolically associated with *the yeast*; now they turn to the undisputed purity of a Jewish way of life, associated in the Passover with unleavened bread. The Christian must be more than, not less than, a Jew. *So let us 'keep the feast' with no trace of the yeast of the old life.*

Vs 9–13 In my previous letter I said, 'Don't mix with the immoral.' I didn't mean, of course, that you were to have no contact at all with the immoral of this world, nor with any cheats or thieves or idolaters – for that would mean going out of the world altogether! But in this letter I tell you not to associate with any professing Christian who is known to be an impure man or a swindler, an idolater, a man with a foul tongue, a drunkard or a thief. My instruction is: 'Don't even eat with such a man.' Those outside the church it is not my business to judge. But surely it is your business to judge those who are inside the church – God alone can judge those who are outside. It is your plain duty to expel this wicked man from your fellowship!

Paul refers back to his first letter which we have lost. What he said in that letter has been misunderstood. He had told them to separate themselves from immoral men. He has now to explain that what he meant was for church discipline, not everyday life. If they separated in Corinth from every man who was immoral they would have to begin a monastic life! What he really meant was that the church must maintain a standard of life which included the discipline of separation. Here the rule is strict, and Paul quotes his earlier letter: '*Don't even eat with such a man.*' It would be cruel and wrong to use this, as some have, to divide families. Paul is not calling for separation, but for discipline. *But surely it is your business to judge those who are inside the church.* On this ground he orders and argues that it is their *plain duty to expel this wicked man from your fellowship* – for the sake of the church as well as for his sake.

Vs 1–8 When any of you has a grievance against another, aren't you ashamed to bring the matter to be settled before a pagan court instead of before the church? Don't you know that Christians will one day judge the world? And if you are to judge the world do you consider yourselves incapable of settling such infinitely smaller matters? Don't you also know that we shall judge the very angels themselves – how much more then matters of this world only! In any case, if you find you have to judge matters of this world, why choose as judges those who count for nothing in the church? I say this deliberately to rouse your sense of shame. Are you really unable to find among your number one man with enough sense to decide a dispute between one and another of you, or must one brother resort to law against another and that before those who have no faith in Christ! It is surely obvious that something must be seriously wrong in your church for you to be having lawsuits at all. Why not *let* yourself be wronged or cheated? Instead of that you cheat and wrong your own brothers.

The divisions in Corinth had become a scandal. They were not even confined to the meetings of the church, but allowed to become public knowledge and in this way bring discredit upon the church. Paul had heard of litigation. He does not complain that their litigation is worse than others, but only that it should take place at all among Christians. The church should be able to demonstrate to the world a new quality of life and they should therefore be able to settle their own disputes. Of course, disputes will arise. A man may feel that he is being cheated even by a fellow-Christian. Then he should act within the church and not go to civil courts. There is here no criticism of the quality of civil courts, only that Christians should need them. The church should be able to handle its own affairs, which involves all relations between Christians. They should be ashamed to take such things to a pagan court, as though pagans could know more of right and wrong in matters of human relationships than Christians do. It is difficult to apply this teaching directly today, because the church itself has greatly influenced the courts. They cannot properly be called pagan courts. Yet the teaching remains. In any matter of personal relations between Christians there should be no resort to the courts. The church itself should be able to deal with disputes of this kind and use its much greater powers of Christian love and forgiveness than any court can use. In matters involving human relations, and this applies specially to disputes in marriage, the church and not the courts should deal with the matter. After Paul's first appeal to their sense of shame, he goes on to point out their future role as rulers of the world and comes down to the simple matter of Christian ethics. It is, after all, much better to be wronged than to exact punishment. If you are afraid that the church might be too soft with him, then prefer to be wronged rather than to wrong him. Because by going to the civil courts *you yourself do him wrong, for you cheat him of Christian love and forgiveness*. How often we have seen divorce courts inflame the hatred between Christians when pastoral care could have reconciled or accepted the separation of incompatibles without vicious recriminations. Paul's words are still wise: *aren't you ashamed to bring the matter to be settled before a pagan court instead of before the church?*

Vs 9–11 Have you forgotten that the kingdom of God will never belong to the wicked? Don't be under any illusion – neither the impure, the idolater or the adulterer; neither the effeminate, the pervert or the thief; neither the swindler, the drunkard, the foul-mouthed or the rapacious shall have any share in the kingdom of God. *And such were some of you!* But you have cleansed yourselves from all that, you have been made whole in spirit, you have been justified in the name of the Lord Jesus and in the Spirit of our God.

This little epilogue to the matter adds nothing but does clear up a possible misunderstanding. He is still thinking of *the immoral man*. He is not advising that the church be soft. He has already referred to a power which the courts do not have. Apart from forgiveness, the churches also have the power of excommunication: *the kingdom of God will never belong to the wicked*. Paul reminds them that the kind of sins which exclude from the kingdom of God, such as that persistently committed by *the immoral man*, are the sins of which they too were once guilty. Such sins cannot be judged in court, they can be forgiven. If they are not forgiven, there is no other way of dealing with them. No amount of arguing in court or punishment can remove the stain of persistent guilt. The church can neither tolerate persistent and immoral behaviour, nor can it hand a man over for trial to a pagan court. It can forgive the man or, if he refuses forgiveness, exclude him. Now Paul approaches the most difficult and most easily misunderstood of all his teaching – the liberty of a Christian man:

Vs 12–20 As a Christian I *may* do anything, but that does not mean that everything is good for me. I may do everything, but I must not be a slave of anything. Food was meant for the stomach and the stomach for food; but God has no permanent purpose for either. But you cannot say that our physical body was made for sexual promiscuity; it was made for the Lord, and in the Lord is the answer to its needs. The God who raised the Lord from the dead will also raise us mortal men by his power. Have you not realized that your bodies are integral parts of Christ himself? Am I then to take parts of Christ and join them to a prostitute? Never! Don't you realize that when a man joins himself to a prostitute he makes with her a physical unity? For, God says, 'the two shall be one flesh'. On the other hand, the man who joins himself to the Lord is one with him in spirit.

Avoid sexual looseness like the plague! Every other sin that a man commits is done outside his own body, but this is an offence against his own body. Have you forgotten that your body is the temple of the Holy Spirit, who lives in you and is God's gift to you, and that you are not the owner of your own body? You have been bought, and at a price! Therefore bring glory to God in your body.

There are no binding rules for a Christian. He cannot say that such and such behaviour is forbidden. The great Christian ethic is total freedom. This is what Augustine summed up as 'Love God and do as you will.' It is dangerous teaching, particularly to a young church brought out of the loose morality of pagan Corinth. But Paul cannot deny his principle. This is what the gospel is about – total freedom. There must appear some contradiction in this total freedom when put beside Paul's insistence that *the immoral man* should be excluded from the church. In this passage he tries to deal with the contradiction. It is a continuing tension. The Christian cannot settle for a set of rules, he must have freedom from the law. In this he is nearer to the 'hippy' than he would like to think. But the church must stand out as an example of how life should be lived, and therefore a very real discipline, self-imposed, is evolved. Paul does this, not on the basis of 'that act is wrong', but on a theological foundation of astonishing originality. He declares *that your bodies are integral parts of Christ himself.* This allows him to attack promiscuous sexual behaviour on the grounds that the joining of the body of Christ to a prostitute is unthinkable. He has a hard time dealing with sex at all, but he gives fairly clear lines for its responsible use. He sees it as a religious act – for a Christian. There is no talk here of the sanctity of marriage, but of the attitude of a man to his body. A Christian is joined to Christ physically. This means that what a man does with his body is more important than what he does with his property. There is no doubt that Paul had his rules, based upon his own Jewish upbringing, but he does not impose these. It is not his method to attack actions, but to describe the effect of actions and leave the Christian in his freedom to make his own responsible decisions.

The gospel is, however, good news, and the ray of hope which shines in this passage is real. A man may almost destroy himself by his perverse behaviour, but because he is joined to the Lord, *the God who raised the Lord from the dead will also raise mortal men.* One need hardly say that by 'man' Paul also means 'woman'. In Christ there is neither male nor female, all are one in Christ. This itself was a revolutionary enough idea.

Chapter 7

Vs 1-11 Now let me deal with the questions raised in your letter.

It is a good principle for a man to have no physical contact with women. Nevertheless, because casual liaisons are so prevalent, let every man have his own wife and every woman her own husband. The husband should give his wife what is due to her as his wife, and the wife should be as fair to her husband. The wife has no longer full rights over her own person, but shares them with her husband. In the same way the husband shares his personal rights with his wife. Do not cheat each other of normal sexual intercourse, unless of course you both decide to abstain temporarily to make special opportunity for prayer. But afterwards you should resume relations as before, or you will expose yourselves to the obvious temptation of Satan.

I give the advice above more as a concession than as a command. I wish that all men were like myself, but I realize that everyone has his own particular gift from God, some one thing and some another. Yet to those who are unmarried or widowed, I say definitely that it is a good thing to remain unattached, as I am. But if they have not the gift of self-control in such matters, by all means let them get married. It is better for them to be married than to be tortured by unsatisfied desire.

To those who are already married my command, or rather, the Lord's command, is that the wife should not be separated from her husband. But if she is separated from him she should either remain unattached or else be reconciled to her husband. A husband must not desert his wife.

Until this point Paul appears to be dealing with what he has heard – disturbing reports from Chloe's people or others who have come to him with news of Corinth. Now he turns to questions they have themselves raised and which they want answered. It would have helped considerably if we had had a copy of that letter to which he refers – *Now let me deal with the questions raised in your letter.*

The first questions concern sex. Paul and the Corinthians appear to agree that the ideal is continence even within marriage. He is probably quoting them when he says that *It is a good principle for a man to have no physical contact with women.* He cannot mean that sexual intercourse itself is wrong, but only that in the present circumstances this is a good rule to follow. We need to look closely at what these 'present circumstances' are and how far they can apply in other ages. First, within marriage. Paul allows a concession. Without changing from his first stated principle, he says that the present state of the world makes it better to marry than to be subject to all kinds of immoral temptations: *let every man have his own wife.* Paul is arguing against casual relationships, because these lower the value of sexual intercourse. At once we see that Paul is far from condemning sexual intercourse as a bad thing. He wishes to raise it to a religious act. Absolute celibacy could be a very high doctrine of sex, abstaining because it is too holy. Once marriage has been admitted, then sexual intercourse should take place. *Do not cheat each other of normal sexual intercourse.* When a man has chosen his wife he should live with her, normally and naturally, remembering that both are joined to the body of the Lord. The only reason he admits for denying sexual intercourse is for spiritual reasons, a kind of fasting mutually agreed. After the fasting, *resume relations as before*. Paul turns now to another aspect of the question, probably because the Corinthians had raised it in this context. What of young widows? Obviously Paul would prefer them to adopt a life of abstinence, but he realizes that this is not always possible. He therefore advises them to marry. *It is better for them to be married than to be tortured by unsatisfied desire*. The next question which clearly follows upon this is derived from the obviously accepted attitude that pagans and Christians have different views of sex. Is this difference so great that it is impossible for a Christian man or woman to live with a pagan partner? Paul says, No. If there is to be a separation it must come from the pagan side.

Vs 12–17   To other people my advice (though this is not a divine command) is this. If a brother has a non-Christian wife who is willing to live with him he should not leave her. A wife in a similar position should not leave her husband. For the unbelieving husband is consecrated by being joined to the person of his wife; the unbelieving wife is similarly consecrated by the Christian brother she has married. If this were not so then your children would bear the stains of paganism, whereas they are actually consecrated to God.

But if the unbelieving partner decides to separate, then let there be a separation. The Christian partner need not consider himself bound in such cases. Yet God has called us to live in peace, and after all how can you, who are a wife, know whether you will be able to save your husband or not? And the same applies to you who are a husband.

I merely add to the above that each man should live his life with the gifts that the Lord has given him and in the condition in which God has called him. This is the rule I lay down in all the churches.

Paul is very careful to show that it is possible to live with a pagan partner, but that if either he or she should seek a separation the Christian should understand. Neither Christian husband nor Christian wife can be sure of winning over the pagan partner. Therefore, while Paul firmly maintains that the Christian should not divorce simply because the partner is a pagan, he does leave the door open for a pagan husband or wife to separate if they cannot bear the Christian! The Corinthians were worried about the children, and Paul has a word for them. He does not argue, but just assumes that the children of a mixed marriage will inevitably follow the road of the Christian parent. On this he bases his argument that the marriage can be blessed by the Christian partner, whether husband or wife. This matter of mixed marriages must have been a real problem in Corinth where the church was a small minority and almost all the converts came from pagan homes. Paul may call for a certain amount of separation, but while this world lasts he wants Christians to live responsibly in it. *This is the rule*, he says, *I lay down in all the churches.*

Vs 18–24 For example, if a man was circumcised when God called him he should not attempt to remove the signs of his circumcision. If on the other hand he was uncircumcised he should not become circumcised. Being circumcised or not being circumcised, what do they matter? The great thing is to obey the orders of God. Everyone should continue in the state in which he heard the call of God. Were you a slave when you heard the call? Don't let that worry you, though if you find an opportunity to become free you had better take it. But a slave who is called to life in Christ is set free in the eyes of the Lord. Similarly a man who was free when God called him becomes a slave – to Christ himself! You have been redeemed, at tremendous cost; don't therefore sell yourselves as slaves to men! My brothers, let every one of us continue to live his life with God in the state in which he was when he was called .

One further example of this rule. Paul's battle against the necessity of circumcision had already become notorious. He makes clear that he is not against circumcision, only against using it as a condition of salvation. *The great thing is to obey the orders of God.* This is really a digression used to illustrate his main point, which is that the Christian should *continue to live his life with God in the state in which he was when he was called.* This sounds like the most reprehensible conservatism – no change! But we need to see it in the setting of a generation which believed that the return of Christ was near. One reaction to this was anarchy; it doesn't really matter, nothing lasts. But it is essential that the Christians should find a responsible way of living in this interim period. The rule is, keep close to your conversion. Running after new ideas, trying to make sure that you have everything, trying new things may be all right for periods of slow change, but in this special period continue in the state in which you were called – circumcised or uncircumcised, married or unmarried, etc. But this rule of no change is difficult to maintain, and when Paul begins to apply it he runs into trouble. He is wise enough to recognize the difference between giving advice and quoting the Lord:

Vs 25-35 Now as far as young unmarried women are concerned, I must confess that I have no direct commands from the Lord. Nevertheless, I give you my considered opinion as of one who is, I think, to be trusted after all his experience of God's mercy.

My opinion is this, that amid all the difficulties of the present time you would do best to remain just as you are. Are you married? Well, don't try to be separated. Are you separated? Then don't try to get married. But if you, a man, should marry, don't think that you have done anything sinful. And the same applies to a young woman. Yet I do believe that those who take this step are bound to find the married state an extra burden in these critical days, and I should like to spare you that. All our futures are so fore-shortened, indeed, that those who have wives should live, so to speak, as though they had none! There is no time to indulge in sorrow, no time for enjoying our joys; those who buy have no time to enjoy their possessions, and indeed their every contact with the world must be as light as possible, for the present scheme of things is rapidly passing away. That is why I should like you to be free from worldly anxieties. The unmarried man is free to concern himself with the Lord's affairs, and how he may please him. But the married man is sure to be concerned also with matters of this world, that he may please his wife – his interests are divided. You find the same difference in the case of the unmarried and the married woman. The un-married concerns herself with the Lord's affairs, and her aim in life is to make herself holy, in body and in spirit. But the married woman must concern herself with the things of this world, and her aim will be to please her husband.

I tell you these things to help you; I am not putting difficulties in your path but setting before you an ideal, so that your service of God may be as far as possible free from worldly distractions.

The sum total of this advice is that in present circum-stances it is really better not to marry. The near approach of the end of the present age puts a question mark over all institutions. Even marriage will not continue into the new age. The Christian is thus advised not to involve himself or herself in any more of the present situation than is strictly necessary. *Amid all the difficulties of the present time you would do best to remain just as you are.* This leads to Paul's assessment of the married state and it is difficult to find this very helpful, except under the special circumstances of the time of writing and the limited attitude to marriage of his day. He would have taken a quite different view if he had spoken today in the very different atmosphere of companionship and co-operation in marriage. Paul limits the married state too much to a cure for sexual promiscuity and makes heavy weather of the burdens of serving each other. In other places he begins to glimpse the possible enrichment of true marriage, but this is not his best subject! He does, however, see that his advice might well lead to a form of cruelty among those who love each other. He at once adds that marriage is not wrong!

Vs 36–40   But if any man feels he is not behaving honourably towards the woman he loves, especially as she is beginning to lose her first youth and the emotional strain is considerable, let him do what his heart tells him to do – let them be married, there is no sin in that. Yet for the man of steadfast purpose who is able to bear the strain and has his own desires well under control, if he decides not to marry the young woman, he too will be doing the right thing. Both of them are right, one in choosing marriage and the other in refraining from marriage, but the latter has chosen the better of two right courses.

A woman is bound to her husband while he is alive, but if he dies she is free to marry whom she likes – but let her be guided by the Lord. In my opinion she would be happier to remain as she is, unmarried. And I think I am here expressing not only my opinion, but the will of the Spirit as well.

There is no doubt that Paul considers the choice of celibacy as the better choice. He will not make that a law nor claim the authority of the Holy Spirit for his advice, but he thinks that the Holy Spirit might agree with him!

Paul now turns to a problem raised in the letter written to him, one which was common enough in any pagan city where sacrifices were frequent. Not all the animals brought for sacrifice were burnt at the altar. The amount of meat left over was considerable. There were two ways of disposing of the surplus meat: the man who sacrificed the animal could invite his friends to join him in a feast; or the priests could dispose of it to the local butcher. In either case, the Christian faced a real problem. He would probably not accept an invitation to the temple for a feast, but some might even consider that a harmless procedure, more social than religious. The second was more difficult. When a Christian went to the market, would he carefully inquire whether the meat had been sacrificed to idols or not? There were obviously two points of view. One party said, 'These idols are nothing, therefore we might as well enjoy the meat', amused at the scruples of others. The other party said, 'If we eat this meat we are in danger of coming again under the domination of idols.' Here is how Paul faced the problem:

Vs 1-13 Now to deal with the matter of food which has been sacrificed to idols. It is easy to think that we 'know' over problems like this, but we should remember that while this 'knowing' may make a man look big, it is only love that can make him grow to his full stature. For if a man thinks he 'knows' he may still be quite ignorant of what he ought to know. But if he loves God he is the man who is known to God.

In this matter, then, of eating food which has been offered to idols, we are sure that no idol has any real existence, and that there is no God but one. For though there are so-called gods both in heaven and earth, gods and lords galore in fact, for us there is only one God, the Father, from whom everything comes, and for whom we live. And there is one Lord, Jesus Christ, through whom everything exists, and through whom we ourselves are alive. But this knowledge of ours is not shared by all men. For some, who until now have been used to idols, eat the food as food really sacrificed to a god, and their delicate conscience is thereby injured. Now our acceptance by God is not a matter of food. If we eat it, that does not make us better men, nor are we the worse if we do not eat it. You must be careful that your freedom to eat food does not in any way hinder anyone whose faith is not as robust as yours. For suppose you with your knowledge of God should be observed eating food in an idol's temple, are you not encouraging the man with a delicate conscience to do the same? Surely you would not want your superior knowledge to bring spiritual disaster to a weaker brother for whom Christ died? And when you sin like this and damage the weak consciences of your brethren, you really sin against Christ. This makes me determined that, if there is any possibility of food injuring my brother, I will never eat food as long as I live, for fear I might do him harm.

While Paul agrees with those who say that there is no harm done in eating what is sacrificed to idols, he also understands the man with scruples and he lays squarely on the shoulders of those whose *faith is robust* or who claim to have *superior knowledge* the responsibility of choosing between exercising their *freedom* or causing *spiritual disaster* to those who have *weak consciences*. The matter can be settled by the question, 'Shall we be guided by superior knowledge or by love for the brethren?' He clearly considers that it is better not to exercise his freedom if thereby he might harm the conscience of another. This cannot be applied in simplicity. It must be thought out carefully and a balance found, because there are very few things which would not harm somebody in some circumstances. Paul is for freedom, but carefully guarded by a love for our fellow-believers who do not always think as we do.

There were other parts to this letter from Corinth which dealt not only with questions that needed answering, but reports that needed correcting. Some in Corinth doubted Paul's authority. He was not an original disciple like Peter and his teaching occasionally seemed to clash with that of Jerusalem. He spoke as though he had absolute authority over them and yet some wanted to question his theology, his ethical advice and his attitude to Corinth. There is ample evidence of discontent with Paul. He deals with this delicately. He must establish his claim to be a true apostle and to have special authority over Corinth. Remember, no bishops are yet appointed and no church organization is able to determine orthodoxy. In Acts 15 there is an account of some primitive form of church council, but all is so far in the beginning, and the strong sense that Christ would soon return leads to some negligence in setting up a rigid authority. Paul has, therefore, to argue for his.

Vs 1–6 Is there any doubt that I am a free man, any doubt that I am a genuine messenger? Have I not seen Jesus our Lord with my own eyes? Are not you yourselves samples of my work for the Lord? Even if other people should refuse to recognize my divine commission, yet to you at any rate I shall always be a true messenger, for you are a living proof of the Lord's call to me. This is my real ground of defence to those who cross-examine me.

Aren't we allowed to eat and drink? May we not travel with a Christian wife like the other messengers, like other

Christian brothers, and like Cephas? Are Barnabas and I the only ones not allowed to leave their ordinary work to give time to the ministry?

His claims are that he is *a free man, a genuine messenger*. This is based upon the fact that he has *seen the Lord*, i.e. that he is a witness of the resurrection. Paul regarded the vision on the Damascus road as a genuine resurrection appearance. He then comes nearer home with the argument that their existence as a church is evidence of his genuine apostolic ministry. Others may doubt it, but so long as they are a church of Jesus Christ, they should not. The doubts seem to have arisen in relation to the fact that Paul does not depend upon them for support. He does not impose a wife upon their hospitality – as apparently Peter does – he works with his hands and supports himself. This applies equally to Barnabas. He drives the point home that a preacher of the gospel has a right to be supported, much as a soldier is supported when he goes to war.

Vs 7–12 Just think for a moment. Does any soldier ever go to war at his own expense? Does any man plant a vineyard and have no share in its fruits? Does the shepherd who tends the flock never taste the milk? This is, I know, an argument from everyday life, but it is a principle endorsed by the Law. For is it not written in the Law of Moses:

> Thou shalt not muzzle the ox when he treadeth out the corn?

Now does this imply merely God's care for oxen, or does it include his care for us too? Surely we are included! You might even say that the words were written for us. For both the ploughman as he ploughs, and the thresher as he threshes should have some hope of an ultimate share in the harvest. If we have sown for you the seed of spiritual things need you be greatly perturbed because we reap some of your material things? And if there are others with the right to have these things from you, have not we an even greater right? Yet we have never exercised this right and have put up with all sorts of things, so that we might not hinder the spread of the gospel.

With these arguments there can be no doubt that Paul as a preacher of the gospel has as much right as the shepherd tending the flock or the ox treading the corn to have his share. As he pushes this into the field of sacred things, he explains why he has not taken these privileges.

Vs 13-15 Are you ignorant of the fact that those who minister sacred things take part of the sacred food of the Temple for their own use, and those who attend the altar have their share of what is placed on the altar? On the same principle the Lord has ordered that those who proclaim the gospel should receive their livelihood from those who accept the gospel.

But I have never used any of these privileges, nor am I writing now to suggest that I should be given them. Indeed, I would rather die than have anyone make this boast of mine an empty one!

It is difficult to excuse the charge of boasting here! Paul is not saying that Peter is less than him because he takes some support from the churches. He is saying that Paul is no less because he does not. Yet Paul really glories in the fact that he is offering the gospel free! Not that he is without a reward. The fact that he makes the gospel free to all men is a reward.

Vs 16-23 For I take no special pride in the fact that I preach the gospel. I feel compelled to do so; I should be utterly miserable if I failed to preach it. If I do this work because I choose to do so then I am entitled to a reward. But if it is no choice of mine, but a sacred responsibility put upon me, what can I expect in the way of reward? This, that when I preach the gospel I can make it absolutely free of charge, and need not claim what is my rightful due as a preacher. For though I am no man's slave, yet I have made myself everyone's slave, that I might win more men to Christ. To the Jews I was a Jew that I might win the Jews. To those who were under the Law I put myself in the position of being under the Law (although, in fact, I stand free of it), that I might win those who are under the Law. To those who had no Law I myself became like a man without the Law (even though in fact I cannot be a lawless man for I am bound by the law of Christ), so that I might win the men who have no Law. To the weak I became a weak man, that I might win the weak. I have, in short, been all things to all sorts of men that by every possible means I might win some to God. I do all this for the sake of the gospel; I want to play my part properly.

Paul forfeits all his rights for the sake of proclaiming the gospel to all men and freely. But he loses track of the argument as he tells of his desire to be faithful. His images take over as he sees himself competing in a race or fighting a fight. It is a real race, and no shadow-boxing:

Vs 24–27 Do you remember how, on a racing-track, every competitor runs, but only one wins the prize? Well, you ought to run with your minds fixed on winning the prize! Every competitor in athletic events goes into serious training. Athletes will take tremendous pains – for a fading crown of leaves. But our contest is for a crown that will never fade.

I run the race then with determination. I am no shadow-boxer, I really fight! I am my body's sternest master, for

c.c.   c

fear that when I have preached to others I should myself be disqualified.

There is just a trace of real concern, which every minister has felt at one time or another – *for fear that . . . I should myself be disqualified.*

Chapter 10

The high calling of a Christian which Paul has emphasized could lead to a sense of arrogance and false confidence. Writing like a rabbi, Paul draws upon the Old Testament to show that not all the people of God are worthy. His treatment of the Old Testament is a little fanciful, but in the best tradition of a rabbi of his day. In this passage he is at his most Jewish:

Vs 1–12 For I should like to remind you, my brothers, that our ancestors all had the experience of being guided by the cloud in the desert and of crossing the sea dry-shod. They were all, so to speak, 'baptized' into Moses by these experiences. They all shared the same spiritual food and drank the same spiritual drink (for they drank from the spiritual rock which followed them, and that rock was Christ). Yet in spite of all these experiences most of them failed to please God, and left their bones in the desert. Now in these events our ancestors stand as examples to us, warning us not to crave after evil things as they did. Nor are you to worship false gods as they did. The scripture says:

> The people sat down to eat and drink, and rose up to play.

Neither should we give way to sexual immorality as did some of them, for we read that twenty-three thousand fell in a single day! Nor should we dare to exploit the goodness of God as some of them did, and fell victims to poisonous snakes. Nor yet must you curse the lot that God has appointed to you as some of them did, and met their end at the hand of the angel of death.

Now these things which happened to our ancestors are illustrations of the way in which God works, and they were written down to be a warning to us who are living in the final days of the present order.

So let the man who feels sure of his standing today be careful that he does not fall tomorrow.

The style of this passage at once warns the reader that Paul has turned away from arguing or simply answering questions. *For I should like to remind you, my brothers.* What follows is an attempt to draw parallels from the Old Testament story. It is not an historical treatment, but what is called 'typological', i.e. the Old Testament stories are used as 'types' of the 'events' in the life of Christ and in the experience of the Christian. All the people of God shared the miraculous and spiritual experiences, but not all inherited the promises. Paul is, in fact, saying that spiritual experience is no guarantee of Christian fulfilment. This is a direct blow at the common assumption that one who has become a Christian and is *baptized* is safe! It may seem an elaborate argument to us, but at least Paul comes quite clear at the end. *So let the man who feels sure of his standing today be careful that he does not fall tomorrow.*

He hesitates after that argument, because it could undermine the confidence of a conscientious Christian. It is all very well attacking the arrogant, but what of those who are already fearful of falling from grace? With a sure hand Paul moves in to comfort:

V 13   No temptation has come your way that is too hard for flesh and blood to bear. But God can be trusted not to allow you to suffer any temptation beyond your powers of endurance. He will see to it that every temptation has its way out, so that it will be possible for you to bear it.

Paul does not want to minimize the spiritual privilege of being a Christian, but he wants the Corinthians to realize the danger they are in by their pride and not to presume too much. There is ample evidence that they think Paul regards them as under-developed intellectually. He has said already that he cannot feed them meat, he has taunted them as babes who need milk! Now, in this serious matter of spiritual pride, he appeals to their much vaunted intelligence – *as intelligent men, use your judgment*.

Vs 14–22 The lesson we must learn, my brothers, is at all costs to avoid worshipping a false god. I am speaking to you as intelligent men: use your judgment over what I am saying.

The cup of blessing which we bless, is it not a very sharing in the blood of Christ? When we break the bread do we not actually share in the body of Christ? The very fact that we, many as we are, share one bread makes us all one body. Look at the Jewish people. Isn't there a fellowship between all those who eat the altar sacrifices?

Now, am I implying that a false god really exists, or that sacrifices made to any god have some value? Not at all! I say emphatically that gentile sacrifices are made to evil spiritual powers and not to God at all. I don't want you to have any fellowship with such powers. You cannot drink both the cup of the Lord and the cup of devils. You cannot be a guest at the Lord's table and at the table of devils. Are we trying to arouse the wrath of the Lord? Do we think we are stronger than he?

The *false god* is not, of course, an idol in the usual pagan sense. The Corinthian Christians would not worship such. There follows a very beautiful and precious account of how the early Christians regarded the Holy Communion. This is the contrast with the *false god*. And to their horror the Corin-

thians must have realized that he *was* referring to the worship
of pagan gods. He is back at the question of eating meat
sacrificed to idols. Those of more robust consciences regard
the pagan gods as no gods. So does Paul. But these sacrifices
are real sacrifices. Whether the gods exist or not, their influence is powerful enough. There was enough parallel between
the Christian sacrament and the pagan sacrifice for Paul to
denounce any attempt to combine the two. Here he is showing the real fear of *the man with a delicate conscience*. The eating of
meats offered to idols or the joining in a pagan festival
destroys such a man's participation at the Holy Communion.
Paul realizes that he is getting nowhere with those who take
a liberal view. They are not moved by arguments about
the wrath of the Lord. So he returns to his stronger line, love, not
knowledge, is to be the guiding principle.

Vs 23-33 As I have said before, the Christian position is
this: I may do anything, but everything is not useful. Yes,
I may do anything, but everything is not constructive. Let
no man, then, set his own advantage as his objective, but
rather the good of his neighbour.

Eat whatever is sold in the meat-market without any
question of conscience. The whole earth and all that is in
it belongs to the Lord.

If a pagan asks you to dinner and you want to go, feel
free to eat whatever is set before you, without asking any
questions through conscientious scruples. But if someone
should say straight out, 'This has been offered to an idol',
then don't eat it, for his sake – I mean for the sake of
conscience, not yours but his.

Now why should my freedom to eat be at the mercy of
someone else's conscience? Or why should any evil be said
of me when I have eaten food with gratitude and have
thanked God for it? Because, whatever you do, eating or

drinking or anything else, everything should be done to bring glory to God.

Do nothing that might make men stumble, whether they are Jews or Greeks or members of the church of God. I myself try to be agreeable to all men without considering my own advantage but that of the majority, that if possible they may be saved.

The practical advice, then, is to behave as though you did not know what has happened to the meat. If it doesn't worry you, then don't ask questions. Paul does not expect the Corinthian Christian with a robust faith to be forever seeking out trouble. But if, without asking, a troubled brother should say, '*This has been offered to an idol*', then for the sake of his conscience *don't eat it*. That is sound enough advice, but the problem obviously troubled Paul, who would have liked to say that a Christian was free to do as he pleased, laughing at the idols which are no-gods. He understands the plea for freedom. But in his own life too, he was prepared to limit his own freedom rather than hinder the gospel. This is the apostle, the champion of freedom, yet ever ready to be all things to all men, that he might win some! A Christian can eat and drink even food offered to idols, to the glory of God. There is no limitation of freedom, except the limitation of love. *Do nothing that might make men stumble*. He adds, *whether they are Jews or Greeks*, because he is not only talking about those of the *church of God*. Accept the morality of others, not as a burden, limiting your freedom, but as an act of love, *that if possible they may be saved*.

And he has reason to add at the head of the next chapter, *Copy me*, because this has been the pattern of his own behaviour.

Chapter 11

First a little left over from the last chapter:

V 1 Copy me, my brothers, as I copy Christ himself.

There are some strange traditions which have entered into Christian behaviour. One generation does not easily accept the morality of an earlier day. This applies equally to another culture. The naked African must have wondered why the missionaries put him into trousers! Paul has to explain some traditions which have passed into Christianity from Judaism.

Vs 2–16 I must give you credit for remembering what I taught you and adhering to the traditions I passed on to you. But I want you to know that Christ is the head of every individual man, just as a man is the 'head' of the woman and God is the head of Christ. If a man prays or preaches with his head covered, he is dishonouring his own head. But in the case of a woman, if she prays or preaches with her head uncovered it is just as much a disgrace as if she had had it closely shaved. For if a woman does not cover her head she might just as well have her hair cropped. And if to be cropped or closely shaven is a sign of disgrace to women, then that is all the more reason for her to cover her head. A man ought not to cover his head, for he represents the very person and glory of God, while the woman reflects the glory of the man. For man does not exist because woman exists, but vice versa. Man was not created originally for the sake of woman, but woman was created for the sake of man. For this reason a woman ought to bear on her head an outward sign of man's authority for all the angels to see.

Of course, in the sight of the Lord neither 'man' nor 'woman' has any separate existence. For if woman was made originally from man, no man is now born except by a woman, and both man and woman, like everything else, owe their existence to God. But use your own judgment: do you think it right and proper for a woman to pray to God bare-headed? Isn't there a natural principle here, that makes us feel that long hair is disgraceful to a man, but of glorious beauty to a woman? We feel this because the long hair is the cover provided by nature for the woman's head. But if anyone wants to be argumentative about it, I can only say that we and the churches of God generally hold this ruling on the matter.

The influence of this passage is seen every time a woman puts a handkerchief over her head before entering a church! Few would accept Paul's reasons for covering the head of a woman, and he himself does not appear to be very convinced by his arguments. At the end he simply says, *use your own judgment*. He does not mean that the Corinthians can do as they please, but that surely they will recognize that it is not *right and proper for a woman to pray to God bare-headed*. We need not stay by his reasons. They carry little weight today, although the influence of the decision is persistent. The importance of this rule is that some order should pertain in Corinth. They were a disorderly lot and even little rules can be important if they remind the worshippers of the need for respect. We do not smoke in church, but we might be hard put to explain why. Paul is anxious to maintain respect, and in this he is a child of his time and of his upbringing as a Jew in Tarsus. Another kind of Jew might have insisted upon men covering the head, for similar reasons.

Paul develops a hierarchy of creation: God, man, woman. If that is disturbed, much harm may come. He does not subordinate women by this, but he does insist that all have their place. Good order in the church is his real aim. To maintain this there must be a distinction between man and woman. But, *of course, in the sight of the Lord, neither 'man' nor 'woman' has any separate existence.* There is a complete sex equality in his thinking. Paul is clearly troubled by the reasons he has given for the practice of covering the woman's head or veiling. He comes at last to, *Isn't there a natural principle here?* Or, if they do not feel there is and, if his previous shaky arguments do not convince them, then the Christians of Corinth must learn that there are other Christians throughout the world and if they want *to be argumentative about it*, they must simply accept that *we and the churches of God generally hold this ruling on the matter.* This is Paul at his weakest! He hurries on to more serious disorders:

Vs 17–22 But in giving you the following rules, I cannot commend your conduct, for it seems that your church meetings do you more harm than good! For first, when you meet for worship I hear that you split up into small groups, and I think there must be truth in what I hear. (I grant that you must be able to make choices or your best men might go unrecognized.) But, as it is, when you are assembled in one place you do not eat the *Lord's* supper. For everyone tries to grab his food before anyone else, with the result that one goes hungry and another has too much to drink! Haven't you houses of your own to have your meals in, or are you showing contempt for the church of God and causing acute embarrassment to those who have no other home?

What do you expect from me? Compliments? Certainly not on this!

From earliest times there had been two elements in the Communion Service. On the one hand, it was, after all, a meal, and some Christians, as at Corinth, took this literally. Yet it was also a solemn occasion for worship. When the meal element predominated there was danger of irreverence. Paul heard of worse. The behaviour at the Communion meal was not only unseemly, it contradicted the very teaching of communion. *For everyone tries to grab his food before anyone else.* This rebuke leads Paul to quote the primitive memory of the church about that first Last Supper:

Vs 23–29   The teaching I gave you was given me personally by the Lord himself, and it was this: the Lord Jesus, in the same night in which he was betrayed, took bread and when he had given thanks he broke it and said, 'This is my body – and it is for you. Do this in remembrance of me.' Similarly, when supper was ended, he took the cup saying, 'This cup is the new agreement made by my blood: do this, whenever you drink it, in remembrance of me.'

This can only mean that whenever you eat this bread and drink this cup, you are proclaiming the Lord's death until he comes again. So that, whoever eats the bread or drinks the cup of the Lord without proper reverence is sinning against the body and blood of the Lord.

No, a man should thoroughly examine himself, and only then should he eat the bread or drink of the cup. He that eats and drinks carelessly is eating and drinking a condemnation of himself, for he is blind to the presence of the Body.

This is the earliest account of the Last Supper which we possess. This letter was written about A.D. 56. But this is what he had told them when first he preached in Corinth and instructed the new Christians. He goes back further even than that. *The teaching I gave you was given me.* And he claims an

authority for it which is more than that of tradition. Certainly
he got this account from the first disciples after his conversion, but he claims that he received it *personally* from *the
Lord himself*. Paul uses this highest authority to say that there
is an element in the Communion Service of the church
which is more than a love feast. By repeating the very words
used on the first occasion, the Christians are both doing
something which is more than words, as a *remembrance*, whatever that word means; and they are *proclaiming the Lord's death
until he comes*. The Lord's Supper is both a remembering and a
looking forward. The power which at the moment of
Communion is in the hands of the believer is such that he
must do this thing with great care. This is not just a celebra-
tion, but the most solemn moment of the church's worship.
For this reason a man must *thoroughly examine himself* before
partaking. A careless partaking, such as Paul hears was
common enough in Corinth, means being blind to the
presence of *the Body*. He goes on to show the effect of this:

Vs 30–34 It is this careless participation which is the
reason for the many feeble and sickly Christians in your
church, and the explanation of the fact that many of you
are spiritually asleep.

If we were closely to examine ourselves beforehand, we
should avoid the judgment of God. But when God does
judge us, he disciplines us as his own sons, that we may not
be involved in the general condemnation of the world.

Now, my brothers, when you come together to eat this
bread, wait your proper turn. If a man is really hungry
let him satisfy his appetite at home. Don't let your communions be God's judgment upon you!

The other matters I will settle in person, when I come.

Paul is a little ambiguous as to whether he means spiritual
weakness or actual physical weakness. He may mean both.

Anyway, there is no doubt that the careless attitude to the Communion is responsible for the Corinthians being a bit dim about spiritual discernment. Paul calls it *spiritually asleep*, and the questions he is now dealing with are ample evidence of that dimness! He urges them again to examine themselves carefully and then gives practical advice which really separates the love feast from the Communion. He does this for practical rather than theological reasons. In other better ordered churches it may be possible to include both. In Corinth it is dangerous. *Wait your proper turn* suggests a disorderly congregation! *If a man is really hungry let him satisfy his appetite at home.* Paul is speaking the practical advice of a pastor. He wants their Communions to be for spiritual health, not *God's judgment upon* them.

There are other matters to be dealt with in this list of questions, but Paul intends to visit Corinth and he feels that they can best be dealt with personally. He has been content to treat only the urgent and serious matters which must have direct and practical answers. He turns now to teaching.

Chapter 12

There is a religious phenomenon which is usually described as 'speaking with tongues'. It is not confined to Christianity, but found in many different religions, part of the stock of religious experiences which the early church shared with pagan religions and which persists to this day in one form or another. It usually takes the form of a devotee being possessed by his or her god and falling into a trance. In that state the devotee utters words which may be wildly unintelligible or in a foreign language. There was apparently an outpouring of this 'speaking with tongues' in Corinth. Paul has several related problems to deal with. Is this phenomenon Christian or a survival of paganism? How important is it? Some in Corinth thought that all Christians should speak with tongues. Finally, how can this abundance of spiritual energy be poured into useful channels? How can this phenomenon be put into perspective? Paul has a mammoth task!

Vs 1–11 Now, my brothers, I want to give you some further information in spiritual matters. You have not forgotten that you are gentiles, following dumb idols just as your impulses led you. Now I want you to understand, as Christians, that no one speaking by the Spirit of God could say, 'a curse on Jesus', and no one could say, 'Jesus is Lord', except by the Holy Spirit.

Men have different gifts, but it is the same Spirit who gives them. There are different ways of serving God, but it is the same Lord who is served. God works through different men in different ways, but it is the same God who achieves his purposes through them all. The Spirit openly makes his gift to each man, so that he may use it for the common good.

One man's gift by the Spirit is to speak with wisdom, another's to speak with knowledge. The same Spirit gives to another man faith, to another the ability to heal, to another the use of spiritual powers. The same Spirit gives to another man the gift of preaching the word of God, to another the ability to discriminate in spiritual matters, to another speech in different tongues, and to yet another the power to interpret the tongues. Behind all these gifts is the operation of the same Spirit, who distributes to each individual man, as he wills.

'Speaking with tongues' can be pagan. Paul could not forget that they had been *gentiles, following dumb idols*. Clearly, if a man is possessed by a spirit and cries out in a trance uttering, '*a curse on Jesus*', then the phenomenon is pagan. But sometimes those 'speaking with tongues' had blessed Jesus, crying out, '*Jesus is Lord*'. It was difficult to deny that such praise did not come from the Spirit of God.

But *men have different gifts* and it is important for the Corinthians to see that all were equally important, equally signs of God's presence. Behind all these gifts, and Paul manages to slip in *the power to interpret the tongues*, is the power of God. He argues for variety and uses a well-known analogy, the parts of the human body:

Vs 12–26   As the human body, which has many parts, is a unity, and those parts, despite their multiplicity, constitute one single body, so it is with Christ. For we were all baptized by the one Spirit into one body, whether we were Jews, Greeks, slaves or free men, and we have all had experience of the same Spirit.

Now the body is not one part but many. If the foot should say, 'Because I am not a hand I don't belong to the body,' does that alter the fact that the foot *is* a part of the body? Or if the ear should say, 'Because I am not an eye I don't belong to the body,' does that mean that the ear really is no part of the body? After all, if the body were all one eye, for example, where would be the sense of hearing? Or if it were all one ear, where would be the sense of smell? But God has arranged all the parts in the one body according to his design. For if everything were concentrated in one part, how could there be a body at all? The fact is there are many parts, but only one body. So that the eye cannot say to the hand, 'I don't need you!' nor, again, can the head say to the feet, 'I don't need you!' On the contrary, those parts of the body which seem to have less strength are more essential to health: and to those parts of the body which seem to us to be less admirable we have to allow the highest honour of function. The parts which do not look beautiful have a deeper beauty in the work they do, while the parts which look beautiful may not be at all essential to life! But God has harmonized the whole body by giving importance of function to the parts which lack apparent importance, that the body should work together as a whole with all the members in sympathetic relationship with one another. So it happens that if one member suffers all the other members suffer with it, and if one member is honoured all the members share a common joy.

Paul was hardly original in that analogy, but it fits beautifully what he now wants to say. He has moved skilfully from a human body to the body of Christ and on to the Church, which is the body of Christ. Now he makes the point directly:

Vs 27–28 Now you are together the body of Christ, and each of you is a part of it. And in the Church God has appointed first some to be his messengers, secondly, some to be preachers of power, thirdly teachers. After them he has appointed workers of spiritual power, men with the gift of healing, helpers, counsellors and those with the gift of speaking various 'tongues'.

Those Corinthian Christians who have attached so much importance to the spectacular gift of 'speaking with tongues' must now see how absurd it would be if this was all the Church had. His next questions are rhetorical:

Vs 29–30 As we look at the body of Christ do we find all are his messengers, all are preachers, or all teachers? Do we find all wielders of spiritual power, all able to heal, all able to speak with tongues, or all able to interpret the tongues?

Of course, one needs a variety of gifts, but if there are not some spectacular gifts which are better than others, are there not grades? Yes, says Paul, and he promises to tell them about the best of all:

V 31 You should set your hearts on the best spiritual gifts, but I will show you a way which surpasses them all.

In the next chapter, to their surprise, he shows that 'love' is the gift that surpasses them all.

Chapter 13

Is there more to say than just to listen to the words of this chapter? One can imagine the Corinthians hearing it for the first time. They had argued about their superior spiritual gifts. They had even suspected that one who did not speak with tongues was hardly a Christian. What did they not have, these eloquent men?

Vs 1–3 If I speak with the eloquence of men and of angels, but have no love, I become no more than blaring brass or crashing cymbal. If I have the gift of foretelling the future and hold in my mind not only all human knowledge but the very secrets of God, and if I also have that absolute faith which can move mountains, but have no love, I amount to nothing at all. If I dispose of all that I possess, yes, even if I give my own body to be burned, but have no love, I achieve precisely nothing.

In one blow Paul has reduced their spectacular gifts to size and shown that only love makes any gift of value. This was the gift they seemed to lack and they must have felt small as he reduced their eloquence, their prophecy, their knowledge, their spiritual insights, their miracles, their ostentatious sacrifice and so much else to 'nothing without love'.

But what is this love of which he speaks and which Corinth seems to lack?

Vs 4–8a This love of which I speak is slow to lose patience – it looks for a way of being constructive. It is not posses-

sive: it is neither anxious to impress nor does it cherish
inflated ideas of its own importance.

Love has good manners and does not pursue selfish
advantage. It is not touchy. It does not keep account of
evil or gloat over the wickedness of other people. On the
contrary, it shares the joy of those who live by the truth.

Love knows no limit to its endurance, no end to its
trust, no fading of its hope; it can outlast anything. Love
never fails.

In this way Paul has made love into a person, perhaps a
portrait of Jesus himself, as Paul imagined him to be. Certainly this person is the very opposite of the typical Corinthian
as he emerges from Paul's criticism of him. And love will
last, *it can outlast anything*. Paul's time scale is short. He expects
the present order to come to an end soon. His question now
is, what will last into the new age? He cannot see prophecy,
speaking with tongues, knowledge, all the gifts the Corinthians most admire, lasting on into the new age:

Vs 8b–10   For if there are prophecies they will be fulfilled
and done with, if there are 'tongues' the need for them will
disappear, if there is knowledge it will be swallowed up in
truth. For our knowledge is always incomplete and our
prophecy is always incomplete, and when the complete
comes, that is the end of the incomplete.

If these things, held in such high esteem now, will not last,
what kind of an age are we approaching? Paul uses the
analogy of growing up:

Vs 11–12   When I was a little child I talked and felt and
thought like a little child. Now that I am a man I have
finished with childish things.

At present we are men looking at puzzling reflections in
a mirror. The time will come when we shall see reality

whole and face to face! At present all I know is a little fraction of the truth, but the time will come when I shall know it as fully as God has known me!

His final summary needs no comment:

V 13 In this life we have three lasting qualities – faith, hope and love. But the greatest of them is love.

But he is not yet finished with 'speaking with tongues'. The next chapter has much to say.

Chapter 14

If love is to be the touchstone of all spiritual gifts, then 'speaking with tongues' has to be looked at again. What use is it? Does it help my fellow-man?

Vs 1-5 Follow, then, the way of love, while you set your heart on the gifts of the Spirit. The highest gift you can wish for is to be able to speak the messages of God. The man who speaks in a 'tongue' addresses not men (for no one understands a word he says) but God: and only in his spirit is he speaking spiritual secrets. But he who preaches the word of God is using his speech for the building up of the faith of one man, the encouragement of another or the consolation of another. The speaker in a 'tongue' builds up his own soul, but the preacher builds up the Church.

I should indeed like you all to speak with 'tongues', but I would much rather that you all preached the word of God. For the preacher of the word does a greater work than the speaker with 'tongues', unless of course the latter interprets his words for the benefit of the Church.

The argument is convincing. If you are judging gifts by their usefulness to others, rather than by their spectacular nature, 'tongues' comes low down on the list. The value of 'tongues' is their usefulness.

Vs 6-11 For suppose I come to you, my brothers, speaking with 'tongues', what good could I do you unless I could give you some revelation of truth, some knowledge in spiritual things, some message from God, or some teaching about the Christian life?

Even in the case of inanimate objects which are capable of making sound, such as a flute or harp, unless their notes have the proper intervals, who can tell what tune is being played on them? Unless the bugle-notes are clear, who will be called to arms? So, in your case, unless you make intelligible sounds with your 'tongue', how can anyone know what you are talking about? You might just as well be addressing an empty room!

There may be in the world a great variety of spoken sounds and none is without meaning. But if the sounds of the speaker's voice mean nothing to me I am bound to sound like a foreigner to him, and he like a foreigner to me.

He is moving now towards some form of pastoral advice. How shall we judge the value of a gift? The richest gift is that which builds up the church. If the Corinthians are really anxious to have the best gifts then let them revise their standards of judgment:

Vs 12–19 So, with yourselves, since you are so eager to possess spiritual gifts, concentrate your ambition upon receiving those which make for the real growth of your church. And that means if one of your number speaks with a 'tongue', he should pray that he may be able to interpret what he says.

If I pray in a 'tongue' my spirit is praying but my mind is inactive. I am therefore determined to pray with my spirit *and* my mind, and if I sing I will sing with both spirit and mind. Otherwise, if you are praising God with your spirit, how can the uninstructed man say amen to your thanksgiving, since he does not know what you are talking about? You may be thanking God splendidly, but it doesn't help the other man at all. I thank God that I have a greater gift of 'tongues' than any of you, yet when I am in church I would rather speak five words with my mind (which might teach something to other people) than ten thousand words in a 'tongue' which nobody understands.

This argument by Paul has prevailed. In those churches where 'speaking with tongues' is common and highly valued, there is a strong emphasis on the 'tongues' being understood and, therefore, almost invariably an 'interpreter' speaks after the 'tongues'. Paul goes further in his insistence upon the greater usefulness of the mind. He does not condemn speaking with tongues, in fact he claims to be better at it than any of them, but he prefers words that can be understood and edify the church. In fact, he urges them to use their minds in this matter of tongues:

Vs 20–25 My brothers, don't be children but use your intelligence! By all means be innocent as babes as far as evil is concerned, but where your minds are concerned be full-grown men! In the Law it is written:

> By men of strange tongues and by the lips of strangers will I speak unto this people: and not even thus will they hear me, saith the Lord.

That means that tongues are a sign of God's power, not for those who are unbelievers but for those who already believe. Preaching the word of God, on the other hand, is a sign of God's power to those who do not believe rather than to believers. So that, if at a full church meeting you are all speaking with tongues and men come in who are uninstructed or without faith, will they not say that you are insane? But if you are preaching God's word and such a man should come in to your meeting, he is convicted and challenged by your united speaking of the truth. His secrets are exposed and he will fall on his knees acknowledging God and saying that God is truly among you!

In translating Paul's comment on the quotation from Isaiah 28.11–12, J. B. Phillips has departed from the usually accepted Greek text because he believes that here we have either a slip of the pen or a copyist error. The Greek of verse 22 is literally: 'So that tongues are a sign, not to the believers, but to the unbelievers. Prophecy, on the other hand, is not to the unbelievers, but to the believers.' In J. B. Phillips' version the text means that 'tongues' are for mature Christians and not for explaining the word of God to unbelievers. On the literal meaning of the text, we must assume that 'tongues' demonstrated the power of God to unbelievers, who would say, 'surely God was with them', while for believers 'tongues' are quite unnecessary. Prophecy is what believers want. They should use their minds and not depend upon spectacular signs.

J. B. Phillips is supported by what follows. The example given suggests that these tongues would not impress a visitor, who would think them *insane*. It is when he hears true prophecy or *preaching* that *his secrets are exposed* and *he will fall on his knees* and acknowledge *God is truly among you*! Whichever Paul meant, he clearly had no high opinion of 'speaking with tongues', although he would not 'quench the spirit'.

Paul proceeds to give practical advice about how to contain the enthusiasm of these 'tongues'. He gives certain suggested regulations for the exercise of spiritual gifts:

Vs 26–33 Well then, my brothers, whenever you meet let everyone be ready to contribute a psalm, a piece of teaching, a spiritual truth, or a 'tongue' with an interpreter. Everything should be done to make your church strong in the faith.

If the question of speaking with a 'tongue' arises, confine the speaking to two or three at the most. They must speak in turn and have someone to interpret what is said. If you have no interpreter then let the speaker with a 'tongue' keep silent in the church and speak only to himself and God. Don't have more than two or three preachers either, while the others think over what has been said. But should a message of truth come to one who is seated, then the original speaker should stop talking. For in this way you can all have the opportunity to give a message, one after the other, and everyone will learn something and everyone will have his faith stimulated. The spirit of a true preacher is under that preacher's control, for God is not a God of disorder but of harmony, as is plain in all the churches.

This little passage is a precious vignette of life in the early church, which clearly had some difficulty with containing the enthusiasm of its members. Paul insists upon good order and there is a suggestion that he has had experience of the difficulty of controlling women. His comment has never been popular!

Vs 34-35   Let women be silent in church; they are not to be allowed to speak. They must submit to this regulation, as the Law itself instructs. If they have questions to ask they must ask their husbands at home, for there is something improper about a woman's speaking in church.

Despite his careful explanation, he expects them to accept his authority. He has many churches to concern him and he wishes them to retain a reputation for good order, in the face of much opposition from conservative and Jewish elements in the church. One can imagine him defending Corinth when he is in Jerusalem. But talking to Corinth he attacks their tendency to disorder:

Vs 36-40   Are you beginning to imagine that the Word of God originated in your church, or that you have a monopoly of God's truth? If any of your number think himself a true preacher and a spiritually-minded man, let him realize that what I have written is by divine command! If a man does not recognize this he himself should not be recognized.

In conclusion, then, my brothers, set your heart on preaching the Word of God, while not forbidding the use of 'tongues'. Let everything be done decently and in order.

Chapter 15

With some difficulty Paul has extricated himself from the subject of 'speaking with tongues', and perhaps the chapters which have covered this phenomenon in one way or another are the measure of the importance of the problem. But now he would remind them of the gospel which he had preached to them at the first. The summary recalls those sermons in the Acts which C. H. Dodd has recognized as the bare bones of apostolic preaching – the *kerygma*, or what the town-crier calls out after he has blown the trumpet:

> Vs 1–4 Now, my brothers, I want to remind you of the gospel which I have previously preached to you, which you accepted, on which you have taken your stand, and by which, if you remain faithful to the message I gave you, your salvation is being worked out – unless, of course, your faith had no meaning behind it at all.
>
> For I passed on to you – as essential, the message I had myself received – that Christ died for our sins, as the scriptures said he would; that he was buried and rose again on the third day, again as the scriptures foretold.

But the keystone in this arch was the resurrection. Paul gives the evidence, as it was handed down to him:

> Vs 5–7 He was seen by Cephas, then by the twelve, and subsequently he was seen simultaneously by over five hundred Christians, of whom the majority are still alive, though some have since died. He was then seen by James, then by all the messengers.

Most of these can be identified from later accounts in the gospels, except that strange, *he was seen simultaneously by over five hundred Christians*. Paul points this one up with, *of whom the majority are still alive*. So far he is telling them what he has been told – *For I passed on to you* – as essential, *the message I had myself received*. Now he adds his own personal testimony with the same conviction, equally a resurrection appearance:

Vs 8–9 And last of all, as to one born abnormally late, he appeared even to me! I am the least of the messengers, and indeed I do not deserve that title at all, because I persecuted the Church of God.

Without deserving it, he was made an apostle like the rest. The essential qualification for an apostle is that he should have seen Christ, risen from the dead. Paul did not deserve to be an apostle, but Christ appeared to him and this gave him a new authority, that of an apostle:

Vs 10–11 But what I am now I am by the grace of God. The grace he gave me has not proved a barren gift. I have worked harder than any of the others – and yet it was not I but this same grace of God within me. In any event, whoever has done the work, whether I or they, this has been our message and this has been your faith.

His preaching had been the foundation of their faith. So, at least, he was *their* apostle. Paul will never let them escape that. He does not boast, or he feels ashamed of himself when he does, but neither will he allow that his authority as an apostle could be called in question. He stands upon that authority for the sake of the doctrine he preaches and for their sakes, lest anyone should say that they are not fully Christian. What emerges from this is Paul's conviction that *the rising of Christ from the dead is the very heart of* the gospel. He develops this at once:

Vs 12–19 Now if the rising of Christ from the dead is the very heart of our message, how can some of you deny that there is any resurrection? For if there is no such thing as the resurrection of the dead, then Christ was never raised. And if Christ was not raised then neither our preaching nor your faith has any meaning at all. Further, it would mean that we are lying in our witness for God, for we have given our solemn testimony that he did raise up Christ – and that is utterly false if it should be true that the dead do not, in fact, rise again! For if the dead do not rise neither did Christ rise, and if Christ did not rise your faith is futile and your sins have never been forgiven. Moreover, those who have died believing in Christ are utterly dead and gone. Truly, if our hope in Christ were limited to this life only we should, of all mankind, be the most to be pitied!

One detects already the question which the Corinthians had raised about the fate of those who had died while they were waiting for the return of Christ. He will deal more fully with that later. Now he goes on to assert his faith:

Vs 20–28 But the glorious fact is that Christ was raised from the dead: he has become the very first to rise of all who sleep the sleep of death. As death entered the world through a man, so has rising from the dead come to us through a man! As members of a sinful race all men die; as members of Christ all men shall be raised to life, each in his proper order, with Christ the very first and after him all who belong to him when he comes.

Then, and not till then, comes the end when Christ, having abolished all other rule, authority and power, hands over the kingdom to God the Father. Christ's reign will and must continue until every enemy has been conquered. The last enemy of all to be destroyed is death itself. The scripture says:

He hath put all things in subjection under his feet.
But in the term 'all things' it is quite obvious that God, who
brings them all under subjection to Christ, is himself
excepted. Nevertheless, when everything has been made
subject to God, then shall the Son himself be subject to
God, who gave him power over all things. Thus, in the
end, shall God be wholly and absolutely God.

If the resurrection is the heart of the gospel, how can any
Christian deny that those who died are risen to another life
beyond death? He then uses a very strange argument:

V 29   Further, you should consider this, that if there is
to be no resurrection, what is the point of some of you
being baptized for the dead by proxy? Why should you be
baptized for *dead bodies*?

What does this mean? We can only conclude that the
Corinthians had some kind of practice, similar to that the
Mormons follow today, of being baptized for those who have
died. Paul is obviously assembling all the arguments he knows
to reduce a disbelief in the resurrection to absurdity. He has
looked at their strange practice and said that they obviously
must believe in the resurrection of the dead or they are
behaving stupidly in being *baptized for dead bodies*! Now he turns
to his own sufferings and endurance. Are these for nothing?

Vs 30–32   And why should we live a life of such hourly
danger? I assure you, by the proud certainty which we
share in Christ Jesus our Lord, that I face death every day
of my life! And if, to use the popular expression, I have
'fought with wild beasts' here in Ephesus, what is the good
of an ordeal like that if there is no life after this one? Let
us rather eat, drink and be merry, for tomorrow we die!

A literal translation of Paul's strange reference would be,

'If, as a man, I fought with wild beasts at Ephesus, what use was that to me?' It is unlikely that he actually fought with wild beasts in the arena and lived, but he may be using a metaphor for his guards in prison or, as J. B. Phillips suggests, this was a well-known saying for being taken into custody by the authorities – *And if, to use the popular expression, I have 'fought with wild beasts'*. The point is clear. Christian endurance has little value unless we can look beyond this life. Paul is ashamed that he has to make these obvious points. Corinthian Christians have apparently suffered from the company they have been keeping:

Vs 33–34 Don't let yourselves be deceived. It is true that 'evil communications corrupt good manners'. Come back to your right senses, and stop sinning like this! Remember that there are men who have no knowledge of God. You should be ashamed that I have to write like this!

While he cannot understand why any Christian can doubt the fact of the resurrection, either of Christ or Christians, he can sympathize with those who have difficulty with understanding how it can happen. The same questions have always been asked about the resurrection of the dead. Where do all the bodies go? Shall we recognize one another after death? But even these questions are met with a little scorn. *Now that is a silly question!* He deals with it, however, by drawing parallels from nature:

Vs 35–50 But perhaps someone will ask, 'How is the resurrection achieved? With what sort of body do the dead arrive?' Now that is a silly question! In your own experience you know that a seed does not germinate without itself 'dying'. When you sow a seed you do not sow the 'body' that will eventually be produced, but bare grain, of wheat, for example, or one of the other seeds. God gives the seed

a 'body' according to his laws – a different 'body' to each
kind of seed.

Then again, all flesh is not identical. There is a difference
in the flesh of human beings, animals, birds and fish.

There are bodies which exist in the heavens, and bodies
which exist in this world. The splendour of an earthly body
is quite a different thing from the splendour of a heavenly
body. The sun, the moon and the stars all have their own
particular splendour; and one star differs from another in
splendour.

There are illustrations here of the raising of the dead.
The body is 'sown' in corruption; it is raised beyond the
reach of corruption. It is 'sown' in dishonour; it is raised
in splendour. It is sown in weakness; it is raised in power.
It is sown a natural body; it is raised a spiritual body. As
there is a natural body so will there be a spiritual body.

It is written, moreover, that:

The first man Adam became a living soul.

So the last Adam is a life-giving Spirit. But we should
notice that the 'spiritual' does not come first: the order is
'natural' first and then 'spiritual'. The first man came out
of the earth, a material creature; the second man came
from heaven. For the life of this world men are made like
the material man; but for the life that is to come they are
made like the one from heaven. So that just as we have
been made like the material pattern, so we shall be made
like the heavenly pattern. For I assure you, my brothers,
it is utterly impossible for flesh and blood to possess the
kingdom of God. The transitory could never possess the
everlasting.

All that is perfectly reasonable and calmly argued. Its
point can be taken still. But there are yet more serious
questions. What about the teaching of the return of Christ?

Where will the dead be when he comes? Is it a disaster to die before Christ comes? Will you miss the show? One suspects that many godly leaders in Corinth had already died and death became a frightening kind of loss. It may be true that we live after death, but what of the resurrection day? What happens to those who have died already and where do they meet the living on that day? These were puzzling questions, and Paul, already convinced that the return of Christ may well be delayed, attempts to deal with them:

Vs 51-58 Listen, and I will tell you a secret. We shall not all die, but suddenly, in the twinkling of an eye, every one of us will be changed as the last trumpet sounds! For the trumpet will sound and the dead shall be raised beyond the reach of corruption, and we shall be changed. For this perishable nature of ours must be wrapped in imperishability, these bodies which are mortal must be wrapped in immortality. So when the perishable is lost in the imperishable, the mortal lost in the immortal, this scripture will come true:

Death is swallowed up in victory.

Where now, O death, is your victory; where now is your stinging power? It is sin which gives death its sting, and it is the Law which gives sin its power. All thanks to God, then, who gives us the victory over these things through our Lord Jesus Christ!

And so, brothers of mine, stand firm! Let nothing move you as you busy yourselves in the Lord's work. Be sure that nothing you do for him is ever lost or ever wasted.

In that section he does more than answer some dated questions. He gives a new page to the liturgy of the church, which has comforted and inspired generations since, and still does today.

Chapter 16

This is a very practical letter and the contrast between the resurrection and the collection may not have seemed so sharp to Paul at it does to us! He is still dealing with questions raised by representatives from Corinth. We know from Acts 11.27-30 that there had been a real shortage of food in Jerusalem and that Christians throughout the world had rallied to the need of their brethren. This seems to have become a regular tribute of the gentile churches to their Jewish parents, and some in Corinth were querying the procedure. Paul has had to deal with similar questions in the Galatian churches and he repeats the same advice here. When Paul fought for the freedom of the gentile churches in Jerusalem at the Council described in Acts 15, one of the treaty agreement terms was *that we should not forget the poor* (Galatians 2.10). Paul raises the question here:

> V 1 Now as far as the fund for Christians in need is concerned, I should like you to follow the same rule that I gave to the Galatian church.

But it is typical of this letter that he also spells out the practical details, such as apparently he had given to the Galatians.

> Vs 2-9 On the first day of the week let everyone put so much by him, according to his financial prosperity, so that there will be no need for collections when I come. Then, on my arrival, I will send whomever you approve to take your gift, with my written recommendation, to Jerusalem.

If it seems right for me to go as well, we will make up a party together. I shall come to you after my intended journey through Macedonia and I may stay with you awhile or even spend the winter with you. Then you can see me on my way – wherever it is that I go next. I don't wish to see you now, for it would merely be in passing, and I hope to spend some time with you, if it is the Lord's will. I shall stay here in Ephesus until the feast of Pentecost, for I have been given a great opportunity of doing useful work, and there are many against me.

This passage got Paul into trouble later. He is much concerned with his next visit to Corinth. He does not want a hurried visit – *I don't wish to see you now, for it would merely be in passing* – because that might deepen the misunderstanding. But his promise of a longer visit, which he did not keep, led to criticism. More of that in 2 Corinthians. Meanwhile, he has plans to ask Timothy to go to Corinth on his way to meeting Paul in Ephesus. Again we shall hear more of this letter, but Paul must already be aware that Timothy would not be accepted as a substitute for himself:

Vs 10–12 If Timothy comes to you, put him at his ease. He is as genuine a worker for the Lord as I am, and there is therefore no reason to look down on him. Send him on his way in peace, for I am expecting him to come to me here with the other Christian brothers. As for our brother Apollos, I pressed him strongly to go to you with the rest, but it was definitely not God's will for him to do so then. However, he will come to you as soon as an opportunity occurs.

Paul assures the Corinthians that he would be quite happy about Apollos coming to them. It was not he who had hindered the visit of this popular preacher. There is a touch of anxiety still in Paul's references to Apollos. As though he were giving them a 'thought for the day', he adds:

Vs 13–14 Be on your guard, stand firm in the faith, live like men, be strong! Let everything that you do be done in love.

Paul ends this letter as so often he does with personal references. They can never mean as much to us today as once they meant to the first readers:

Vs 15–20 Now I have a request to make of you, my brothers.
  You remember the household of Stephanas, the first men of Achaia to be won for Christ? Well, they have made up their minds to devote their lives to looking after Christian brothers. I do beg you to recognize such men, and to extend your recognition to anyone who works and labours with them.
  I am very glad that Stephanas, Fortunatus and Achaicus have arrived. They have made up for what you were unable to do. They have relieved my anxiety and yours. You should appreciate having men like that!
  Greetings from the churches of Asia. Aquila and Prisca send you their warmest Christian greetings and so does the church that meets in their house. All the Christians here send greetings. I should like you to shake hands all round as a sign of Christian love.

J. B. Phillips has modernized the greetings. What in Greek reads, 'Greet one another with a holy kiss', now reads, *shake hands all round as a sign of Christian love*. The kiss of peace was part of Christian worship as early as the second century, and there may be an earlier reference to it here and in Romans 16.16.

Now Paul adds his own greetings, probably in his own hand:

Vs 21–24　Here is my own greeting, written by me, Paul.

'If any man does not love the Lord, a curse be on him; may the Lord soon come!'

The grace of the Lord Jesus be with you and my love be with you all in Christ Jesus.

There are allusions to worship here:

1. an exclusion of the unworthy, probably from the Eucharist, '*If any man does not love the Lord, a curse be on him.*'
2. an early prayer left in the original Aramaic, 'maranatha', *may the Lord soon come.* The Greek simply transliterates the original Aramaic here.
3. the grace.

These references would be most telling if we can assume the letter to have been read aloud at worship.

The Second Letter
to the Christians at Corinth

Chapter 1

As has already been explained in the Introduction, this 'second letter' contains all that remains of three separate letters. The earliest is undated, but certainly earlier than our 1 Corinthians. Part of it is preserved in the fragment, 2 Corinthians 6.14–7.1. This is the letter in which Paul said, *'Don't mix with the immoral'*. (1 Corinthians 5.9) It was followed by 1 Corinthians in A.D. 56. The next letter was a 'severe letter' and we shall come to that in 2 Corinthians 10–13. Paul's last letter to the Christians at Corinth is contained in the first nine chapters of the present book. It was written in the summer of A.D. 57.

After a painful rift in the good relations between Paul and his church at Corinth, the apostle waited anxiously for news in Troas. He preached there with an uneasy mind because there was no news of *brother Titus*. He left Troas and came, still anxious, back to Macedonia, where he had the good news that all was well. He wrote, probably from Ephesus:

Vs 1–2   This letter comes to you from Paul, God's messenger for Christ Jesus by the will of God, and from brother Timothy, and is addressed to the church of God in Corinth and all Christians throughout Achaia.

May grace and peace come to you from God our Father and from the Lord Jesus Christ.

Timothy had not been very well received earlier at Corinth when they had expected the apostle, not his deputy! Now peace is restored and Paul associates his colleague with him, *and from brother Timothy*.

The habit is beginning of circulating letters to be read at the hour of worship, for edification. Paul encouraged this when he addressed this letter, not only to Corinth but also to *all Christians throughout Achaia*. This custom accounts for the survival of so many of Paul's letters. After the familiar greeting, Paul gives thanks to God and associates the Christians of Corinth with him in an expression of utter confidence. These opening bursts in Paul's letters usually contain some hint of the subject to be dealt with!

Vs 3–7 Thank God, the Father of our Lord Jesus Christ, that he is our Father and the source of all mercy and comfort. For he gives us comfort in all our trials so that we in turn may be able to give the same sort of strong sympathy to others in their troubles that we receive from God. Indeed, experience shows that the more we share in Christ's immeasurable suffering the more we are able to give of his encouragement. This means that if we experience trouble it is for your comfort and spiritual protection; for if we ourselves have been comforted we know how to encourage you to endure patiently the same sort of troubles that we ourselves endure. We are quite confident that if you have to suffer troubles as we have done, then, like us, you will find the comfort and encouragement of God.

Troubles and suffering are to be taken as a gift from God. They not only give God the opportunity to show his goodness in strengthening us, but they also give us the opportunity to sympathize with and help others. The theme is to be persecution, Paul's and theirs. They are not to seek an easy life, but rather to rejoice when it is hard. The familiar consolation of the sufferer is the hope of a larger destiny in the future. Paul brings that into the present. They are to suffer with Christ. More, their sharing is to console others,

*the more we share in Christ's immeasurable suffering the more we are able
to give of his encouragement.* So the call is not simply to endure
suffering because of the great reward, but to suffer with
Christ, 'to contribute my own sufferings something to the
uncompleted pains which Christ suffers on behalf of his
Body, the Church'. (Colossians 1.24) It is the same argument
here in the Corinthian letter. Paul's sufferings can help them
and theirs can help others. He concludes that he is quite
confident that if they have to suffer as he has done, then they,
like him, *will find the comfort and encouragement of God.* Paul begins
to illustrate his point from something that happened in
Asia:

> Vs 8–11 We should like you, our brothers, to know some-
> thing of the trouble we went through in Asia. At that time
> we were completely overwhelmed, the burden was more
> than we could bear, in fact we told ourselves that this was
> the end. Yet we believe now that we had this sense of
> impending disaster so that we might learn to trust, not in
> ourselves, but in God who can raise the dead. It was God
> who preserved us from such deadly perils, and it is he who
> still preserves us. We put our full trust in him and he will
> keep us safe in the future. Here you can co-operate by
> praying for us, so that the help that is given to us in answer
> to many prayers will mean that many will thank God for
> our preservation.

It is very difficult to discover what this trouble was.
Nothing in the account given in the Acts could possibly
match such serious language. If the disturbances in Ephesus
(Acts 19.23–41) are referred to, then the author of the Acts
must have failed to understand what really happened. This
reference reminds us again of how little we know of Paul's
life. We should have had no reference to this *deadly peril* if
Paul had not used it to illustrate his point that the trouble

taught him how *to trust, not in ourselves, but in God who can raise the dead*. He uses the incident also to teach the value of prayer and the ultimate value of suffering, which leads to many praising *God for our preservation*.

There have been misunderstandings and Paul is anxious to make clear that he would rather deal honestly with the Christians in Corinth. He even uses a word that he often uses in accusation – *pride*. We shall hear a lot about pride in this letter. Paul's first use is of legitimate pride:

> Vs 12-14   Now it is a matter of pride to us – endorsed by our conscience – that our activities in this world, particularly our dealings with you, have been absolutely above-board and sincere before God. They have not been marked by any worldly wisdom, but by the grace of God. Our letters to you have no double meaning – they mean just what you understand them to mean when you read them. I hope you will always understand these letters. Just as I believe that you have partially understood me, so you will come to realize that you can be as honestly proud of us, as we are of you, on the day of the Lord Jesus.

He does not attempt to be clever with them. His letters do not have *double meanings*. He carefully emphasizes this. He has no desire to compete with the rhetoric of Greece. He is a plain man and says exactly what he means. For this reason they can be *proud* of him. He solemnly adds, *as we are of you, on the day of the Lord Jesus*. But can they be proud of him? Some little inconsistency rankles. He had promised to visit them and had apparently chosen another route. Why?

> Vs 15-22   Trusting you, and believing that you trusted us, our original plan was to pay you a visit first, and give you a double 'treat'. We meant to come here to Macedonia after first visiting you, and then to visit you again on leaving here. You could thus have helped us on our way towards

Judaea. Because we had to change this plan, does it mean that we are fickle? Do you think I plan with my tongue in my cheek, saying 'yes' and 'no' to suit my own wishes? We solemnly assure you that as certainly as God is faithful so we have never given you a message meaning 'yes' and 'no'. Jesus Christ, the Son of God, whom Silvanus, Timothy and I have preached to you, was himself no doubtful quantity, he is the divine 'yes'. Every promise of God finds its affirmative in him, and through him can be said the final amen, to the glory of God. Both you and we owe our position in Christ to this God of positive promise: it is he who has consecrated us to this special work, he who has given us the living guarantee of the Spirit in our hearts.

Paul bases his case on the nature of the God he preached. For Paul it is of utmost importance that they should not think of God as double-minded. He is a positive God, not like the double-tongued oracles who tricked their worshippers with words. Both Corinth and Paul himself owe their position *to this God of positive promise*. Such a God would not have an apostle who dealt in double talk. Paul asks them to believe in his honesty on the basis of the kind of God who appointed him and to believe that there was a good reason for abandoning the promised visit. It was not because he did not care for them, but rather because he did not want to hurt them.

Vs 23–24 No, I declare before God – and I would stake my life on it – that it was to avoid hurting you that I did not come to Corinth. We are not trying to dominate you and your faith – your faith is firm enough – but we can work with you to increase your joy.

Chapter 2

The chapter break is artificial. Paul continues from the last verses of the previous chapter.

Vs 1–4 And I made up my mind that I would not pay you another painful visit. For what point is there in my depressing the very people who can give me such joy? The real purpose of my previous letter was, in fact, to save myself from being saddened by those whom I might reasonably expect to bring me joy. I felt sure that my happiness was also yours! I wrote to you in deep distress and out of a most unhappy heart (I don't mind telling you I shed tears over that letter), not, believe me, to cause you pain, but to show you how very deep is my love for you.

Although his actions seemed inconsistent, his motives were in keeping with the principles he had already outlined in his 'first letter'. True, he *did not come to Corinth*, but he made *love for you* his overriding principle. This mattered most and he could express that better in a letter, over which he *shed tears*, than in a stormy visit. The question at stake was his authority. It had been challenged. The letter Paul wrote is preserved in 2 Corinthians 10–13. After he had sent it, he could neither preach nor find peace until he received an answer. He seems to have received that answer and now he calls upon them to forgive the man who has caused all the trouble. He had demanded that the offender be punished, probably excommunicated, and this was *a test* of his authority. Now that his authority has been established and they have expressed their disapproval of the crime, they should forgive the man.

Vs 5–11 If the behaviour of a certain person has caused distress, it does not mean so much that he has injured me, but that to some extent (I do not wish to exaggerate) he has injured all of you. But now I think that the punishment which most of you inflicted on such a man has been sufficient. Now is the time to offer him forgiveness and comfort, so that a man in his position is not completely overwhelmed by remorse. I ask you to assure him now that you love him. My previous letter was something of a test – I wanted to make sure that you would follow my orders implicitly. If you forgive a certain person for anything, I forgive him too. Insofar as I had anything personally to forgive, I do forgive him for your sake, as before Christ. We don't want Satan to win any victory here, and well we know his methods!

Paul cannot easily forget the time he spent waiting for news from Titus, who had gone to Corinth and was to tell him of the reception of the 'severe letter'. Although he now looks back from the secure position of knowing that they had received it well, he remembers that he was not so sure when he went to Troas. There he was anxious for news.

Vs 12–13 Well, when I came to Troas to preach the gospel of Christ, although there was an obvious God-given opportunity, I must confess I was on edge the whole time because there was no sign of brother Titus. So I said good-bye and went from there to Macedonia.

It was in Macedonia that he heard the news. Paul seems to change even as he recounts that critical time. He forgets his narrative and goes on to talk about the Christian missionary.

Vs 14-17 Thanks be to God who leads us, wherever we are, on Christ's triumphant way and makes our knowledge of him spread throughout the world like a lovely perfume! We Christians have the unmistakable 'scent' of Christ, discernible alike to those who are being saved and to those who are heading for death. To the latter it seems like the deathly smell of doom, to the former it has the refreshing fragrance of life itself.

Who is fit for such a task! We are not like that large number who corrupt the Word of God. No, we speak in utter sincerity as men sent by God, Christ's ministers under the eyes of God.

Paul's mind is rich in metaphor – the *triumphant way*, recalling a victor's triumphal procession; *a lovely perfume*, which can hardly fail to be noticed, whether as *the deathly smell of doom* or *the fragrance of life; not like that large number who corrupt the Word of God*, which in the Greek recalls mercenary motives or counterfeit arguments. Paul proclaims, he does not corrupt, he is *under the eyes of God*.

Chapter 3

Paul's claim at the end of the last chapter suggests to him the need for *credentials*. He has claimed that he does not corrupt the Word of God, that he is a man sent by God. Will the Corinthians, who had queried his claim to be an apostle, ask him now for *credentials*?

Vs 1–3 Does this mean yet another production of credentials? Do we need, as some apparently do, to exchange testimonials before we can be friends? You yourselves are our testimonial, written in our hearts and yet open for anyone to inspect and read. You are an open letter about Christ delivered by us and written, not with pen and ink, but with the Spirit of the living God, engraved not on stone, but on human hearts.

The answer is clear enough. Their very existence as a Christian church is Paul's *credentials*. The credentials which an ambassador might present are in the form of a letter written by the king, or at least signed by him. The Corinthians are compared to such a letter. Paul did not write it, but he carries this letter, written by Christ, as his authority, which he will not have challenged. There is a boldness here, but Paul risks the charge of boasting.

Vs 4–6 We dare to say such things because of the confidence we have in God through Christ. Not that we are in any way confident of doing anything by our own resources – our ability comes from God. It is he who makes us competent administrators of the new agreement, concerned

not with the letter but with the Spirit. The letter of the
Law leads to the death of the soul; the Spirit alone can
give it life.

That last contrast leads him on to a comparison with
Moses, a parallel he would hardly dare to use before a Jewish
audience.

Vs 7–11 The administration of the Law which was engraved in stone (and which led in fact to spiritual death)
was so magnificent that the Israelites were unable to look
unflinchingly at Moses' face, for it was alight with heavenly
splendour. Now if the old administration held such
heavenly, even though transitory, splendour, can we not
see what a much more glorious thing is the new administration of the Spirit of life? If to administer a system which
is to end in condemning men had its glory, how infinitely
more splendid is it to administer a system which ends in
making men right with God! And while it is true that the
former glory has been eclipsed by the latter, we do well to
remember that it is eclipsed because the present and
permanent is so much more glorious than the old and
transient.

It is a daring contrast with the glory of the Law, which he
does not deny. The gospel is so much better, *much more glorious
than the old and transient*. Paul dares to compare his ministry
with that of Moses. There is nothing veiled this time, all is
clear. Paul makes good use of Exodus 34. He sees the veil
over the face of Moses as an indication that the Jews never
fully understood the message. Therefore they had failed to
recognize the Christ. Only when they *turn to the Lord* does *the
veil disappear*. For the Christian there is no veil.

Vs 12–18 With this hope in our hearts we are quite frank
and open in our ministry. We are not like Moses, who veiled

his face to prevent the Israelites from seeing its fading glory. But it was their minds really which were blinded, for even today when the old agreement is read to them there is still a veil over their minds – though the veil has actually been lifted by Christ. Yes, even to this day there is still a veil over their hearts when the writings of Moses are read. Yet if they 'turned to the Lord' the veil would disappear. For the Lord to whom they could turn is the Spirit, and wherever the Spirit of the Lord is, men's souls are set free.

But all of us who are Christians have no veils on our faces, but reflect like mirrors the glory of the Lord. We are transformed in ever-increasing splendour into his own image, and this is the work of the Lord who is the Spirit.

Paul sees in this removing of the veil a true Christian freedom.

Paul continues with his image of the veil. All religions have a way of hiding something. In Paul's day there were many 'mystery religions' whose secrets were closely guarded. Knowledge of these 'truths' and ritual acts brought salvation. Paul is anxious to show that there is no such 'mystery' in the Christian religion. He uses the image of the veil over the face of Moses. Its removal gave Christians a freedom the Jew never possessed and an openness which is unknown to the pagan religions. Christian priests have no hidden mysteries and secret formulae:

Vs 1-6 This is the ministry which God in his mercy has given us and nothing can daunt us. We have set our faces against all shameful secret practices; we use no clever tricks, no dishonest manipulation of the Word of God. We speak the plain truth and so commend ourselves to every man's conscience in the sight of God. If our gospel is 'veiled', the veil must be in the minds of those who are spiritually dying. The god of this world has blinded the minds of those who do not believe, and prevents the light of the glorious gospel of Christ, the image of God, from shining on them. For it is Christ Jesus as Lord whom we preach, not ourselves; we are your servants for Jesus' sake. God, who first ordered light to shine in darkness, has flooded our hearts with his light, so that we can enlighten men with the knowledge of the glory of God, as we see it in the face of Christ.

The references can be to his enemies or to current pagan

practices, and Paul probably meant both. The false teachers who discredited Paul in Corinth as well as the pagan oracles can be defined as *manipulating the Word of God*. In contrast, Paul claims that the true Christian preachers *speak the plain truth*. It has always been characteristic of Christian preaching at its best that it was a form of communication, intended to be understood!

There follows a very dangerous argument. If the preaching is not understood, then is it the fault of the preacher or the hearer? Paul makes definite claims. He says that he has been plain enough and that if the hearer cannot understand, *If our gospel is 'veiled'*, then it must be because the hearer does not want to understand, *the veil must be in the minds of those who are spiritually dying*. Paul may have been justified in using this argument, but it is dangerous for his successors to do so. There is certainly truth in the assertion that misunderstanding can be because we do not want to know, but the hearer rather than the preacher should see this truth. Communication is a two-way traffic. A listener may well turn aside from an understanding of the gospel because he will have to take some definite action if he really accepts what is told him. In the language of the day, this was described as *the god of this world has blinded the minds of those who do not believe*. In modern language we should say that it is not the passages we do not understand which give us trouble, but the passages we do understand!

An image has been hovering around all through this argument, the image of *light*. The *veil* hid the *light* of Moses' countenance; *the god of this world has blinded the minds*. Even while he has been using Exodus 34, Genesis 1 has never been far away. One of the three characteristics of the creative power of God described there is *light in darkness*. The preaching of the gospel is like shining the light into the darkness. Only the blind fail to see the light. This creative power of God, Paul claims, has been *flooded* into his heart. Here he does not claim a special position. The light has flooded in for a reason, *so that we can enlighten men*. So he has taken the old symbol which the Jews and the pagans understood, the symbol of light, as a carrier of salvation. He localizes it in *the face of Christ*. This light, not some trick or manipulation or secret, is the power of his gospel.

Paul turns now to the criticism that he cannot be a real apostle because he has been so often worsted. He begins with his gospel:

Vs 7–9   This priceless treasure we hold, so to speak, in common earthenware – to show that the splendid power of it belongs to God and not to us. We are hard-pressed on all sides, but we are never frustrated; we are puzzled, but never in despair. We are persecuted, but are never deserted: we may be knocked down but we are never knocked out!

Relics, whether Christian or pagan, are preserved in lavish caskets, not so the gospel. The apostle was nothing, but he held a treasure, *in common earthenware*. It was important that the receptacle should not steal the glory from the treasure it contained. An *earthenware* pot is a good image for the frail human body. This contrast between the treasure and the poor pot in which it is contained leads Paul to a rhetorical flourish of contrasts. He is *hard-pressed on all sides*, but never *frustrated*. The series of contrasts no doubt draw upon the criticism of his opponents that he is not a very successful apostle. He admits his *hard-pressed* conditions, but argues that his persistence in the face of all this persecution is more typical of a true apostle than prosperity. Jesus had warned his disciples to beware when all men spoke well of them and to glory when they were despised. To the list of failures which are used as a reproach, Paul lists his successes: *never frustrated . . . never in despair . . . never deserted . . . never knocked out!*

He claims that 'the imitation of Christ' is the best way for an apostle, and this means death:

> Vs 10–14 Every day we experience something of the death of Jesus, so that we may also show the power of the life of Jesus in these bodies of ours. Yes, we who are living are always being exposed to death for Jesus' sake, so that the life of Jesus may be plainly seen in our mortal lives. We are always facing physical death, so that you may know spiritual life. Our faith is like that mentioned in the scripture:
> I believed and therefore did I speak.
> For we too speak because we believe, and we know for certain that he who raised the Lord Jesus from death shall also raise us with Jesus. We shall all stand together before him.

Paul has managed to say more than that death leads to life for him. He has in fact taken upon himself the role of suffering for the community! *We are always facing physical death, so that you may know spiritual life*. This is a daring comparison with the suffering servant of Isaiah, with whom Jesus compared himself. The Christian community looks not for a scapegoat, but for an apostle who suffers for them. It is not necessary that the whole Christian community should be persecuted. It is enough that some are persecuted. Thus the patient bearing of suffering enriches the whole community, and this fact enables him to endure. *This is the reason why we never lose heart.*

> Vs 15–18 All this is indeed working out for your benefit, for as more grace is given to more and more people so will the thanksgiving to the glory of God be increased. This is the reason why we never lose heart. The outward man does indeed suffer wear and tear, but every day the inward

man receives fresh strength. These little troubles (which are really so transitory) are winning for us a permanent, glorious and solid reward out of all proportion to our pain. For we are looking all the time not at the visible things but at the invisible. The visible things are transitory: it is the invisible things that are really permanent.

Such an experience of suffering in the body leading to enrichment for others in their spiritual life leads on to a different attitude to transient things. Paul does not despise the body, but he knows that he is more than body. The theme is continued into the next chapter.

Chapter 5

Paul has already established the fact that the body is a frail thing and that you cannot judge a man by what happens to his body. But, particularly for a Jew, the idea of life without a body is almost impossible to conceive. A man is not made up of separate parts – body, soul, mind and spirit. A man is an animated body. The Lord God breathed into a body the breath of life. The Corinthians were Greek, although many of them had come to Christ through the synagogue, and Paul himself, for all his Greek, was a Hebrew of the Hebrews. He would not treat the body lightly or regard death as a liberation of the bird from its cage. Yet he is here approaching a new understanding of death. The Christians had expected to wait for Christ in the body. Now they were dying. Paul begins with a Greek idea of death as the taking down of the tent.

Vs 1–4 We know, for instance, that if our earthly dwelling were taken down, like a tent, we have a permanent house in Heaven, made, not by man, but by God. In this present frame we sigh with deep longing for our heavenly house, for we do not want to face utter nakedness. So long as we are clothed in this temporary dwelling we have a painful longing, not because we want just to get rid of these 'clothes', but because we want to know the full cover of the permanent. We want our transitory life to be absorbed into the life that is eternal.

This is more than the taking down of a tent or the taking off of clothes. In place of the frail tent comes the *permanent house*, while the '*clothes*' we want to take off are replaced by *the full cover*. The frail is only taken away because something more permanent is prepared for us. God is not taking something away and leaving us naked, he is preparing a rich experience for us.

Vs 5–8 Now the power that has planned this experience for us is God, and he has given us the Spirit as a guarantee of its truth. This makes us confident, whatever happens. We realize that being 'at home' in the body means that to some extent we are 'away' from the Lord, for we have to live by trusting him without seeing him. We are so sure of this that we would really rather be 'away' from the body and be 'at home' with the Lord.

But Paul will not be led into the trap of saying that because we are going to be rid of this frail body it does not matter what we do in the body. Many had said that with disastrous consequences. Our personality is so bound up with our body that what we do in it determines our eternal destiny. Now this is no superficial idea of obeying or disobeying certain rules. There are no rules in Paul's gospel. The body must be treated with respect, it must be used to express our best.

Vs 9–10 It is our aim, therefore, to please him, whether we are 'at home' or 'away'. For every one of us will have to stand without pretence before Christ our judge, and we shall each receive our due for what we did when we lived in our bodies, whether it was good or bad.

What we did when we lived in our bodies means simply that the way we used our bodies formed our very selves. Our body is itself our means of communication to others. The only terrors that death can have is our discovery of ourselves. Paul's little digression is over. He has established the fact that

he does not fear death, but that he lives with the *solemn fea*
of God in his mind.

Vs 11–12 All our persuading of men, then, is with this
solemn fear of God in our minds. What we are is utterly
plain to God – and I hope to your consciences as well. No,
we are not recommending ourselves to you again, but we
can give you grounds for legitimate pride in us – if that is
what you need to meet those who are so proud of the
outward rather than the inward qualification.

Paul appears to be arguing all the way! But he is anxious
to get on to something very important which will enable his
readers to find a sure basis for their actions. For Paul there is
no doubt about his basis: *The very spring of our actions is the love of*
Christ. But he will not be content with such a 'religious'
phrase. He must explain exactly what he means by this and
how it works out in practice.

Vs 13–16 If we are 'mad' it is for God's glory; if we are
perfectly sane it is for your benefit. The very spring of our
actions is the love of Christ. We look at it like this: if one
died for all men, then, in a sense, they all died, and his
purpose in dying for them is that their lives should now
be no longer lived for themselves but for him who died
and was raised to life for them. This means that our
knowledge of men can no longer be based on their outward lives (indeed, even though we knew Christ as a man
we do not know him like that any longer).

The argument is fairly clear. There are no human standards
by which to judge a Christian. Neither can a Christian judge
a man by simply observing what he does, far less by what he
says. Paul takes the extreme example of Christ himself. He
does not say whether or not he knew Christ, *as a man*. He does
claim that those who did, have no superior claim to under-

standing him. At this point Paul develops the idea of being
in Christ. It is this which enables him to understand men, it is
this by which he himself must be judged. So radical is the
change that he can be called *a new creation*. To develop so
fundamental a theme almost incidentally is typical of Paul.
He threw off his newly minted theological ideas as though
they were common-place!

Vs 17–18   For if a man is in Christ he becomes a new
person altogether – the past is finished and gone, everything has become fresh and new. All this is God's doing,
for he has reconciled us to himself through Christ; and he
has made us agents of the reconciliation.

He has not only established that a man in Christ is a new
creation, but also the purpose of this creative act – that he
might become an *agent* of reconciliation. An *agent* is not an
initiator; he repeats what has been done by the one he
represents. In this case, he is an agent of God's act of reconciliation.

Vs 19–21   God was in Christ personally reconciling the
world to himself – not counting their sins against them –
and has commissioned us with the message of reconciliation. We are now Christ's ambassadors, as though God were
appealing direct to you through us. For Christ's sake we
beg you, 'Make your peace with God.' For God caused
Christ, who himself knew nothing of sin, actually to *be*
sin for our sakes, so that in Christ we might be made good
with the goodness of God.

It is a powerful argument and few can resist its logic. God
acts in the person of Jesus Christ. Our experience tells us of
the joy of that reconciliation. We were estranged from God
by our own fault. He won us back. Out of the joy we must
represent him so that he may win others. The whole appeal

is personal. Paul does not suggest that a process has to be gone through. He assumes that men are estranged from God and he appeals out of experience, *For Christ's sake we beg you.* His appeal is to let God reconcile them to himself, that they may become *messengers of reconciliation.* In arguing this he uses a startling phrase about Christ: God caused Christ actually to become sin for us. The metaphor is that of a sacrifice. In some way, Christ, who according to Paul was quite without sin, became involved in human sin. He is then sacrificed and like a scapegoat carries our guilt away. Paul's appeal is not to the Corinthians. He assumes that all this has already happened to them, at least most of them! He is giving rather an example of the appeal they must make to the world. It is they who must say, *For Christ's sake we beg you.* They are his fellow-workers in this task.

Chapter 6

Vs 1–10 As co-operators with God himself we beg you, then, not to fail to use the grace of God which you have received. For God's word is:

At an acceptable time I hearkened unto thee,
And in a day of salvation did I succour thee.

Now *is* the 'acceptable time', and this very day *is* the 'day of salvation'.

As far as we are concerned we do not wish to stand in anyone's way, nor do we wish to bring discredit on the ministry God has given us. Indeed, we want to prove ourselves genuine ministers of God whatever we have to go through – patient endurance of troubles, hardship, desperate situations, being flogged or imprisoned; being mobbed, overworked, sleepless and starving; with sincerity, with insight and patience; by sheer kindness and the Holy Spirit; with genuine love, speaking the plain truth, and living by the power of God. Our sole defence, our only weapon, is a life of integrity, whether we meet honour or dishonour, praise or blame. Called 'impostors' we must be true, called 'nobodies' we must be in the public eye. Never far from death, yet here we are alive, always 'going through it' yet never 'going under'. We know sorrow, yet our joy is inextinguishable. We have 'nothing to bless ourselves with', yet we bless many others with true riches. We are penniless, and yet we possess everything.

The chapter division is quite artificial. The argument continues without a break. Paul has clearly shown what an apostle is not. No doubt he has certain pretenders in mind. Christians are not divided into superiors and inferiors. All are *co-operators with God*. The Corinthians are, therefore, urged to draw upon their resources rather than consider their status. Paul comes at last to an attempt at portraying a true apostle. He hesitates, because this is sensitive ground. It would be all too easy to portray himself as the model Christian. Paul's portrait of a Christian shows the ambiguity. He has no defence against calumny other than his own *integrity*; whatever he is accused of, he must act according to his own vocation, he must be an *impostor* and yet *true*, *nobody* and yet *in the public eye*, *never far from death* yet *alive*, knowing *sorrow* yet overcome with *joy, penniless . . . yet we possess everything*. The secret of the Christian attitude to life lies in those paradoxes. A Christian must never depend upon prosperity and yet he must learn how to enjoy it. Many religions have taught men how to live in poverty; only Christianity shows a man how to retain his integrity in prosperity.

After this rhetorical burst, Paul appeals again in the most personal terms to his fellow-Christians at Corinth:

Vs 11–13 Dear friends in Corinth, we are hiding nothing from you and our hearts are absolutely open to you. Any restraint between us must be on your side, for we assure you there is none on ours. Do reward me (I talk to you as though you were my own children) with the same complete candour!

For the next part of his letter it is important to establish this very personal relation – *I talk to you as though you were my own children*. In this mood he warns them against entanglement with pagans:

Vs 14–18 Don't link up with unbelievers and try to work with them. What common interest can there be between goodness and evil? How can light and darkness share life together? How can there be harmony between Christ and the devil? What can a believer have in common with an unbeliever? What common ground can idols hold with the temple of God? For we, remember, are ourselves temples of the living God, as God has said:

I will dwell in them and walk in them:
And I will be their God, and they shall be my people. Therefore
Come ye out from among them and be ye separate, saith the Lord,
And touch no unclean thing;
And I will receive you,
And will be to you a Father,
And ye shall be to me sons and daughters,
Saith the Lord Almighty.

This dangerous passage must be read in the light of conditions at Corinth and not elevated into a general principle of separation. The life of the general population in Corinth was closely tied up with worship at the local temple. It included all manner of things forbidden to Christians. We have already seen how Paul dealt with the problem of eating meat which had been offered to idols (1 Corinthians 8). There were other rites which involved immorality. In fact, the only way in which the accepted Christian standards could be maintained was by separation. A Christian virtually separated himself from the pagan-impregnated society by becoming a Christian. Paul simply underlines this in these verses. They do not apply to society today, at least not to European society which has been moulded, however incompletely, by Christian teaching over many centuries. Paul compares the Christian community in pagan Corinth to the Jewish people in the time of the exile or after their return when the greatest danger was a loss of that unique teaching which the Jewish people carried for all the nations. They had to be separate for the sake of the message they bore. In South Africa the white races applied this argument in their contact with the black races. It may have had some cogency when a small, civilized minority was trying to preserve civilization in the face of primitive peoples. It has led to dire consequences in modern apartheid.

In the heart of this argument for separation from impurity comes the almost casual statement of the basis of all Christian ethics – *we are temples of the living God*. Christians did not oppose pagan temples with nothing, but with the pure temple of their own body, conditioned by the God who dwells there.

V 1 With these promises ringing in our ears, dear friends, let us cleanse ourselves from anything that pollutes body or soul. Let us prove our reverence for God by consecrating ourselves to him completely.

With that one reference back, Paul now deals with the effect of his 'severe letter'. He had been afraid that his very stern letter might have hurt them and he waited anxiously in Macedonia for Titus to bring news. The news was good and Paul can write with ease now.

Vs 2–4 Do make room in your hearts for us! Not one of you has ever been wronged or ruined or cheated by us. I don't say this to condemn your attitude, but simply because, as I said before, whether we meet death or life together you live in our hearts. I talk to you with utter frankness; I think of you with deepest pride. Whatever troubles I have gone through, the thought of you has filled me with comfort and deep happiness.

And now a little personal narration of what happened when Titus arrived.

Vs 5–11 For even when we arrived in Macedonia we found no rest but trouble all round us – wrangling outside and anxiety within. Not but what God, who cheers the depressed, gave us the comfort of the arrival of Titus. And it wasn't merely his coming that cheered us, but the comfort you had given him, for he could tell us of your eagerness to see me, your deep sorrow and keen interest on my behalf. All that made me doubly glad to see him. For although my letter had hurt you I don't regret it now (even if I did at one time). I can see that the letter did upset you, though only for a time, and now I am glad I sent it, not because I want to hurt you but because it made you grieve for things that were wrong. In other words, the result was to make you sorry as God would have had you sorry, and not to make you feel injured by what we said. The sorrow which God uses means a change of heart and leads to salvation without regret – it is the world's sorrow that is such a deadly thing. You can look back now and see how the hand of God was in that sorrow. Look how seriously it made you think, how eager it made you to prove your innocence, how indignant it made you and how afraid! Look how it made you long for my presence, how it stirred up your keenness for the faith, how ready it made you to punish the offender! You have completely cleared yourselves in this matter.

That vivid account tells us a great deal about Paul and his close relations with Corinth. He has been worried, because he obviously went very far in that letter.

If we glance ahead for a moment at chapters 10–13, we shall see part of that 'severe letter'. His style indicates his nervous attitude, almost controlled anger! *I am going to appeal to you personally . . . Do look at things which stare you in the face! . . . I wish you could put up with a little of my foolishness . . . Once more let me advise you not to look upon me as a fool.* And so it goes on.

The tone is quite different now. Paul had been anxious about the way they would receive his rebuke. He knew that he would cause them sorrow and perhaps estrange them from him. All is over and he can now write as much to himself as to them: *You can look back now and see how the hand of God was in that sorrow*, which he had to cause them by this necessary letter. The total effect was to bring them to their senses and even to go out of their way to show that they were innocent, by promptly punishing the offender. But Paul was not primarily interested in the offender.

Vs 12–16 Now I did not write that letter really for the sake of the man who sinned, or even for the sake of the one who was sinned against, but to let you see for yourselves, in the sight of God, how deeply you really do care for us. That is why we now feel so encouraged, and, in addition, our sense of joy was greatly enhanced by knowing what happiness you all gave to Titus by setting his mind at rest. You see, I had told him of my pride in you, and you have not let me down. I have always spoken the truth *to* you, and this proves that my proud words *about* you were true as well. Titus himself has a much greater love for you, now that he has seen for himself the obedience you gave him, and the respect and reverence with which you treated him. I am profoundly glad to have my confidence in you so fully proved.

He was concerned with their reputation! *I have always spoken the truth to you and this* (the way in which they put Titus' and Paul's minds at rest) *proves that my proud words about you were true as well.*

One of Paul's great concerns for his 'gentile' churches was that they should show a generous sympathy for the poor in Jerusalem. He had pledged himself to raise a fund for the distressed Christians there, who suffered because of the famine. Presumably they were cut off from the traditional Jewish relief since they became Christian. This concern for the poor is one of the conditions which was imposed upon Paul at the Jerusalem Conference of Acts 15.

It is important that the Corinthians should show themselves generous in this matter. Paul begins with an account of the generosity of the other gentile churches in 'Macedonia', i.e. Northern Greece.

Vs 1–5 Now, my brothers, we must tell you about the grace that God has given to the Macedonian churches. Somehow, in most difficult circumstances, their over-flowing joy and the fact of being down to their last penny themselves, produced a magnificent concern for other people. I can guarantee that they were willing to give to the limit of their means, yes and beyond their means, without the slightest urging from me or anyone else. In fact, they simply begged us to accept their gifts and so let them share the honour of supporting their brothers in Christ. Nor was their gift, as I must confess I had expected, a mere cash payment. Instead they made a complete dedication of themselves first to the Lord and then to us, because God willed it.

Titus appears to be Paul's agent in this matter of the

collection and he explains that Titus was chosen with some hesitation to do the same at Corinth. The only thing Paul feared was that they might withhold something because it was not Paul himself who came for the gift. They might even withhold because of the severity of *the letter*. But his fears on that score had been proved groundless:

Vs 6–9   Now this has made us ask Titus, who began this task, to complete it by arranging for you to share in this work of generosity. Already you are well to the fore in every good quality – you have faith, you can express that faith in words; you have knowledge, enthusiasm and your love for us. Could you not add generosity to your virtues? I don't give you this as an order. It is only my suggestion, prompted by what I have seen in others of eagerness to help, that here is a way to prove the reality of your love. Do you remember the generosity of Jesus Christ, the Lord of us all? He was rich, yet he became poor for your sakes so that his poverty might make you rich.

His appeal is made at the highest level, the example of Christ himself. He continues arguing with practical good sense which they will understand. Many of his arguments hold good still. It is good to complete a job with the same readiness, *as you showed eagerness to begin*. The important thing is to give what you can, *no one is asked to give what he has not got*. Then the Corinthians are reminded that it is in their own best interest to give generously – *at some future date their plenty may supply your need*!

Vs 10–15   Here is my opinion in the matter. I think it would be a good thing for you, who were the first a year ago to think of helping, as well as the first to give, to carry through what you then intended to do. Finish it, then, as well as your means allow, and show that you can complete what you set out to do with as much readiness as you showed eagerness to begin. The important thing is to be willing to give as much as we can – that is what God accepts, and no one is asked to give what he has not got. Of course, I don't mean that others should be relieved to an extent that leaves you in distress. It is a matter of share and share alike. At present your plenty should supply their need, and then at some future date their plenty may supply your need. In that way we share with each other, as the scripture says,

> He that gathered much had nothing over,
> And he that gathered little had no lack.

This letter comes then with Titus again. He it was who brought the good news of their sensible acceptance of the 'severe letter'. In this exchange, he has seen Paul's deep concern and feels the same himself:

Vs 16–24 Thank God Titus feels the same deep concern for you as we do! He accepts the suggestion outlined above, and in his enthusiasm comes to you personally at his own request. We are sending with him that brother whose services to the gospel are universally praised in the churches. He has moreover been chosen to travel with us in this work of administering this generous gift. It is a task that brings glory to God and demonstrates also our willingness to help. Naturally we want to avoid the slightest breath of criticism in the distribution of their gifts, and to be absolutely above-board not only in the sight of God but in the eyes of men.

With these two we are also sending our brother, of whose keenness we have ample proof and whose interest is especially aroused on this occasion as he has such confidence in you. As for Titus, he is my partner and colleague in your affairs, and both the brothers are official messengers of the churches, a credit to Christ. So do let them see how genuine is your love, and justify my pride in you, so that all the churches may see it.

Paul takes great care to see that the funds are administered honestly and above-board. He will have no breath of scandal. He therefore sends a team and assures them that Titus will be with him in the handing over of the gift, which he expects to be generous.

It is obvious that this gift is very important to Paul. He continues the same theme in the next chapter.

Chapter 9

Vs 1–6 Of course I know it is really quite superfluous for me to be writing to you about this matter of giving to fellow-Christians, for I know how willing you are. Indeed, I have told the Macedonians with some pride that 'Achaia was ready to undertake this service twelve months ago'. Your enthusiasm has consequently stimulated most of them. I am, however, sending the brothers just to make sure that our pride in you is not unjustified and that you are ready, as I said you were. For it would never do if some of the Macedonians were to accompany me on my visit to you and find you unprepared! We (not to speak of you) should be acutely embarrassed, just because we had been so confident in you. This is my reason, then, for urging the brothers to visit you before I come myself, so that they can get your promised gift ready in good time. For I should like it to be a spontaneous gift, and not money squeezed out of you. All I will say is that poor sowing means a poor harvest, and generous sowing means a generous harvest.

Paul is very anxious that he should not be let down by Corinth, which he here refers to as Achaia, the province of which it is the capital. His style reveals an anxiety which is not matched by the meaning of his words – *it is really quite superfluous for me to be writing to you!* He is going to make sure by *sending the brothers.* Although the response to his 'severe letter' is encouraging he still shows some anxiety. He knows the Corinthians all too well and he is not going to let them get out of their promises! So he appeals for a *spontaneous gift*, which is carefully prepared.

This very pointed reminder, which he professes is unnecessary, is supported by proof texts. Here he uses Proverbs 22.8.

But giving helps the giver as well as the one who receives the gift:

Vs 7–14 Let everyone give as his heart tells him, neither grudgingly nor under compulsion, for God loves the man who gives cheerfully. God can give you more than you can ever need, so that you may always have sufficient for yourselves and enough left over to give to every good cause. As the scripture says:

> He hath scattered abroad, he hath given to the poor;
> His righteousness abideth for ever.

He who gives the seed to the sower and bread to eat will give you the seed of generosity to sow and will make it grow into a harvest of good deeds done. The more you are enriched, the more scope will there be for generous giving, and your gifts, administered through us, will mean that many will thank God. For your giving does not end in meeting the wants of your fellow-Christians. It also results in an overflowing tide of thanksgiving to God. Moreover, your very giving proves the reality of your faith, and that means that men thank God that you practise the gospel of Christ that you profess to believe in, as well as for the actual gifts your fellowship makes to them and to others. And yet further, men will pray for you and feel drawn to you because you have obviously received a generous measure of the grace of God.

Thank God, then, for his indescribable generosity to you!

Paul supports this thesis by reference to Psalm 112.9; Isaiah 55.10 and Hosea 10.12. As he is writing to a largely gentile church we must assume either that they came from those 'god fearers' who had been attached to the synagogue before they became Christians, or that a study of the Old Testament was a part of Christian training. It would appear from the texts quoted here and in other parts of the New Testament that the Christians collected certain specific texts for use in proving the claims of Christ and in supporting elements of Christian teaching. Here Paul is being as Jewish as he is being Christian. The ethical standards of the Jews in the first century were a matter for admiration, and it was this which attracted so many of the 'god fearers' to the synagogue. The Christian church took over the ethical teaching of the synagogue and supplied a Christian turn to it. Thus Paul could be fairly sure that when he quoted these texts his readers would understand what he meant.

Apart from the good done to the giver, this generous gift would also be *an overflowing tide of thanksgiving to God*. It would enhance the reputation of the Corinthians themselves. Many were inclined to believe that these gentiles could never become real Christians. This gift would show that they really did *practise the gospel of Christ*, that they professed. Furthermore, when the Jewish Christians – the pillars of the church – hear of this generous gift they will pray for them and recognize that, despite all their arguing and doubts, they have *obviously received a generous measure of the grace of God*.

All that we have of this letter now ends with thanks to God for this *indescribable generosity to you*, i.e. God's generosity to the Corinthians. One is reminded of the Arab custom still, never to thank you for a gift, but to thank God for giving you the power to give the gift!

The rest of 2 Corinthians is given over to the 'severe letter' which was written before these first nine chapters.

Chapter 10

From this point on, 2 Corinthians has a different style. It is an earlier letter, written almost in anger, certainly in severe rebuke. The letter is referred to in 2 Corinthians 7, where we read of how relieved Paul was to hear that they had received his 'severe letter' and understood that it was written for their good and out of love for them. So at this point we turn back the pages to the letter itself. We may read chapters 10–13 as a kind of appendix. You have heard much about this 'severe letter'. The following chapters are a quote from it, not the whole letter, but obviously a substantial part.

Vs 1–6 Now I am going to appeal to you personally, by the gentleness and kindness of Christ himself. Yes, I, Paul, the one who is 'humble enough in our presence but outspoken when away from us', am begging you to make it unnecessary for me to be outspoken and stern in your presence. For I am afraid otherwise that I think I shall have to do some plain speaking to those of you who will persist in reckoning that our activities are on the purely human level. The truth is that, although we lead normal human lives, the battle we are fighting is on the spiritual level. The very weapons we use are not human but powerful in God's warfare for the destruction of the enemy's strongholds. Our battle is to break down every deceptive argument and every imposing defence that men erect against the true knowledge of God. We fight to capture every thought until it acknowledges the authority of

Christ. Once we are sure of your obedience we are ready to punish every disobedience.

Paul's continuing problem with Corinth is the question of his authority. Who is this Paul? Many were loyal to him and even formed a Paul party which he rejected. There must be no parties in the church, all belong to Christ! Criticisms of him seem to have started about his own personal appearance, his style of preaching, his rather poor impression, the kind of criticism which so cruelly and so easily come in a church about its minister. They preferred more eloquent, more clever preachers and leaders who looked like leaders. As for this Paul, said his critics, '*humble enough in our presence but out-spoken when away from us*', he is not fit to be the minister of a great church like Corinth! The immediate cause of this criticism was his first letter, a fragment of which is quoted at 2 Corinthians 6.14–7.1. There he had called upon them to be *separate*, to keep clear of *anything that pollutes body or soul*. We also have a brief quote from that early letter in 1 Corinthians 5.9, '*Don't mix with the immoral.*' When Paul quoted that, he had to explain that what he meant was, *with the immoral* in the church. There are echoes throughout his letters of a problem over whether a certain *immoral man* should be dismissed from the church. Paul asserted his authority and said that the man should be dismissed. That authority was questioned. Paul was not vindictive. As soon as the matter was agreed he proposed forgiving the man. But here he is still arguing for his authority.

Vs 7–11 Do look at things which stare you in the face! So-and-so considers himself to belong to Christ. All right; but let him think again about himself, for we belong to Christ every bit as much as he. You may think that I have boasted unduly of my authority (which the Lord gave me, remember, to build you up not to break you down), but I don't think I have done anything which will make me ashamed. Yet I don't want you to think of me merely as the man who writes you terrifying letters. I know my critics say, 'His letters are impressive and moving, but his actual presence is feeble and his speaking beneath contempt.' Let them realize that we can be just as 'impressive and moving' in person as we are in our letters.

They look upon him as an insignificant man with no moral right to 'lord it' over them. He argues that they are wrong to judge him simply as a man; *the battle we are fighting is on the spiritual level*. He will not, therefore, use merely human arguments. Whether he is an attractive personality or not is quite irrelevant, as is the argument about eloquent preaching. *The very weapons we use are not human*. Of course, Paul uses arguments to *break down* arguments, but he is engaged in a spiritual warfare and his aim is clearly defined: *We fight to capture every thought until it acknowledges the authority of Christ*. Paul dares to claim that when his authority is challenged, the authority of Christ is attacked! Paul is not happy about this role. He does not want to be considered the kind of man who writes angry intolerant letters. His critics have hurt him with their, '*His letters are impressive and moving, but his actual presence is feeble.*' For a moment he boasts that he can be '*impressive and moving*', but he realizes that he is on very uncertain ground. He has descended to the level of his critics and at that level he may not measure up to their standards! What are their standards and how valid are they?

Vs 12–14   Of course we shouldn't dare include ourselves in the same class as those who write their own testimonials, or even to compare ourselves with them! All they are doing, of course, is to measure themselves by their own standards or by comparisons within their own circle, and that doesn't make for accurate estimation, you may be sure. No, we shall not make any wild claims, but simply judge ourselves by that line of duty which God has marked out for us, and that line includes our work on your behalf. We do not exceed our duty when we embrace your interests, for it was our preaching of the gospel which brought us into contact with you.

Now the apostle is on his own ground. The basis of his authority lies in the fact that he brought the gospel to them. There lies his pride.

Vs 15–18   Our pride is not in matters beyond our proper sphere nor in the labours of other men. No, our hope is that your growing faith will mean the expansion of our proper sphere of action, so that before long we shall be preaching the gospel in districts beyond you, instead of being proud of work that has already been done in someone else's province.

But,

He that glorieth let him glory in the Lord.

It is not self-commendation that matters, it is winning the approval of God.

The quotation is from Jeremiah 9.23–24.

Paul has to explain his anxiety and it is lest they should be led away by some facile kind of preaching and lose the gospel. Paul is not a heresy hunter, but he realizes how many facile religions there are current in his day. There are always persuasive preachers to offer what the crowds want. It is not himself that Paul is thinking of. He is concerned for them. He has prepared them like a bride for Christ and he does not want them seduced by another.

Vs 1–4 I wish you could put up with a little of my foolishness – please try! My jealousy over you is the right sort of jealousy, for in my eyes you are like a fresh unspoiled girl whom I am presenting as fiancée to your only husband, Christ himself. I am afraid that your minds may be seduced from a single-hearted devotion to him by the same subtle means that the serpent used towards Eve. For apparently you cheerfully accept a man who comes to you preaching a different Jesus from the one we told you about, and you readily receive a spirit and a gospel quite different from the ones you originally accepted.

But the accusations still hurt. He makes one last bid that he could hold his own against these new preachers!

Vs 5–6 Yet I cannot believe I am in the least inferior to these extra-special messengers. Perhaps I am not a polished speaker, but I do know what I am talking about, and both what I am and what I say is well known to you.

Then it occurs to him that they may have misunderstood

the way in which he refused to be a burden to them, but preached the gospel free. He has boasted of this before now. Perhaps they thought that a free gospel could not be with authority.

Vs 7–10 Perhaps I made a mistake in lowering myself (though I did it to raise you up) by preaching the gospel of God without a fee? As a matter of fact, I was only able to do this by 'robbing' other churches, for it was what they paid me that made it possible to minister to you. Even when I was with you and was hard up, I did not bother any of you. It was the brothers who came from Macedonia who brought me all that I needed. Yes, I kept myself from being a burden to you then, and so I intend to do in the future. By the truth of Christ within me, no one shall stop my being proud of this independence through all Achaia!

This is a personal matter with Paul. He does not condemn those apostles who were supported by their churches. What he really condemns here is those sham apostles who come and trade on the credulity of the Corinthians, simply for money. He is really angry at the thought that his self-support has been misunderstood as a lack of love. He lets fly at the sham apostles.

Vs 11–15 Does this mean that I do not love you? God knows it doesn't, but I am determined to go on doing as I am doing, so as to cut the ground from under the feet of those who would dearly love to be thought of as God's messengers on the same terms as I am. *God's* messengers? They are counterfeits of the real thing, dishonest practitioners masquerading as the messengers of Christ. Nor do their tactics surprise me when I consider how Satan himself masquerades as an angel of light. It is only to be expected that his agents shall have the appearance of ministers of righteousness – but they will get what they deserve in the end.

But he cannot resist a little boast, and he has much to boast of!

Vs 16–27 Once more, let me advise you not to look upon me as a fool. Yet if you do, then listen to what this 'fool' has to make his little boast about.

I am not now speaking as the Lord commands me but as a fool in this business of boasting. Since all the others are so proud of themselves, let me do a little boasting as well. From your heights of wisdom I am sure you can smile tolerantly on a fool. Oh, you're tolerant all right! You don't mind, do you, if a man takes away your liberty, spends your money, takes advantage of you, puts on airs or even smacks your face? I am almost ashamed to say that I never did brave strong things like that to you. Yet in whatever particular they parade such confidence I (speaking as a fool, remember) can do the same.

Are they Hebrews? So am I.

Are they Israelites? So am I.

Are they descendants of Abraham? So am I.

Are they ministers of Christ? I have more claim to this title than they. This is a silly game but look at this list:

I have worked harder than any of them.

I have served more prison sentences!

I have been beaten times without number.

I have faced death again and again.

I have been beaten the regulation thirty-nine stripes by the Jews five times.

I have been beaten with rods three times.

I have been stoned once.

I have been shipwrecked three times.

I have been twenty-four hours in the open sea.

In my travels I have been in constant danger from rivers, from bandits, from my own countrymen, and from pagans. I have faced danger in city streets, danger in the desert, danger on the high seas, danger among false Christians. I have known drudgery, exhaustion, many sleepless nights, hunger and thirst, fasting, cold and exposure.

That is going to take a lot of answering. Paul has borne the burdens of an apostle. Those sham apostles have no such record as this. He presses on. Corinth is not his only concern. He has many churches to care for.

Vs 28-29 Apart from all external trials I have the daily burden of responsibility for all the churches. Do you think anyone is weak without my feeling his weakness? Does anyone have his faith upset without my burning with indignation?

He gives a new turn to his boasting and tells of a strange story of *weakness* – the well-known story of his escape in a basket. It is also told in Acts 9.23–25. Paul adds the detail that the *town governor* had his orders from *King Aretas*, who ruled over the Nabataens from Petra.

Vs 30-33 Oh, if I am going to boast, let me boast of the things which have shown up my weakness! The God and Father of the Lord Jesus, he who is blessed for ever, knows that I speak the simple truth.

In Damascus, the town governor, acting by King Aretas' order, had his patrols out to arrest me. I escaped through a window and was let down the wall in a basket.

Chapter 12

Although Paul does not really think it is *a good thing*, he continues with his boasting. He will not let these sham apostles have all the experiences. We are privileged to hear him talk about a mystical experience which bears all the authentic signs. He describes it with diffidence.

Vs 1–4 I don't think it's really a good thing for me to boast at all, but if I must I will go on to visions and revelations of the Lord himself. I know a man in Christ who, fourteen years ago, had the experience of being caught up into the third Heaven. I don't know whether it was an actual physical experience, only God knows that. All I know is that this man was caught up into paradise. (I repeat, I do not know whether this was a physical happening or not, God alone knows.) This man heard words that cannot, and indeed must not, be put into human speech.

A man in Christ is, of course, Paul, but the strange way of referring to himself is not without meaning. When a man is caught in some unexplainable experience, he is not quite himself. He can only describe it by standing to one side and observing it. This is an unusual sidelight on Paul, the practical theologian. He makes no claims of any miraculous *physical happening*. He does not fully understand what happened to him. But he too had mystical experiences and he is not ashamed to tell of them.

Vs 5–6 I am proud of an experience like that, but I have

made up my mind not to boast of anything personal, except of my weaknesses. If I should want to boast I should certainly be no fool, for I should be speaking nothing but the truth. Yet I am not going to do so, for I don't want anyone to think more highly of me than is warranted by what he sees of me and hears from me.

He wants them to know that he is as good as any of his detractors, but he insists that it is foolish to boast of any experience, except the experience of weakness, which keeps a man humble. He tells us of his own affliction.

Vs 7–10 So tremendous, however, were the revelations that God gave me that, in order to prevent my becoming absurdly conceited, I was given a stabbing pain – one of Satan's angels – to plague me and effectually stop any conceit. Three times I begged the Lord for it to leave me, but his reply has been, 'My grace is enough for you: for where there is weakness, my power is shown the more completely.' Therefore, I have cheerfully made up my mind to be proud of my weaknesses, because they mean a deeper experience of the power of Christ. I can even enjoy weaknesses, insults, privations, persecutions and difficulties for Christ's sake. For my very weakness makes me strong in him.

We have no idea what this *stabbing pain* was. The Greek is very strong and suggests a stave or a thorn. The old phrase 'a thorn in the flesh' was not a bad translation, but it has become trivialized as a phrase. Paul made the great discovery that when prayer is not answered it can lead to new strength. *For my very weakness makes me strong in him.* Paul has said some very important things in this 'boasting passage', but he is already beginning to feel silly. He is angry at the Corinthians for making this boasting necessary.

Vs 11–13 I have made a fool of myself in this 'boasting' business, but you forced me to do it. If only you had had a better opinion of me it would have been quite unnecessary. For I am not really in the least inferior, nobody as I am, to these extra-special messengers. You have had a demonstration of the power God gives to a genuine messenger by his sheer endurance as well as the miracles, signs and works of spiritual power that you saw with your own eyes. What makes you feel so inferior to other churches? Is it because I have not allowed you to support me financially? My humblest apologies for this great wrong!

He has turned their criticism against them. Do they criticize him because they feel inferior? After all, he is 'their' apostle. If he is less than an apostle, they are less than a church! Something has gone wrong and he suspects that the trouble is that he has not allowed them to support him. He returns to the subject.

Vs 14–15 Now I am all ready to visit you for the third time, and I am still not going to be a burden to you. It is you I want – not your money. Children don't have to put by their savings for their parents; parents do that for their children. Consequently I will most gladly spend and be spent for your good utterly. Does that mean that the more I love you the less you love me?

No one can doubt that Paul took no support from them, but some have suggested that he tricked them in some other way. Perhaps he paraded his virtue of not taking anything from them and let his assistants collect it! His only answer to this is to point to Titus who had a high reputation at Corinth.

Vs 16–18 'All right then,' I hear you say, 'we agree that he himself had none of our money.' But are you thinking that I nevertheless was rogue enough to catch you by some trick? Just think. Did I make any profit out of the messengers I sent you? I asked Titus to go, and sent the brother with him. You don't think Titus made anything out of you, do you? Yet didn't I act in the same spirit as he, and take the same line as he did?

It is odd to find Paul shielding himself with Titus, but he is uncertain of their respect for him. It is an embarrassing moment. Yet he plans a third visit to them. He quickly recovers and asserts his authority with dignity.

Vs 19–21 Are you thinking all this time that I am trying to justify myself in your eyes? Actually I am speaking in Christ before God himself, and my only reason for so doing, my dear friends, is to help you in your spiritual life.
For I must confess that I am afraid that when I come I shall not perhaps find you as I should like to find you, and that you will not find me quite as you would like me to be. I am afraid of finding arguments, jealousy, ill-feeling, divided loyalties, slander, whispering, pride and disharmony. When I come again, will God make me feel ashamed of you as I stand among you? Shall I have to grieve over many who have sinned already and are not yet sorry for the impurity, the immorality and the lustfulness of which they are guilty?

The real anxiety about how this letter will be received which we found in 2 Corinthians 7 comes mostly from this section. He hits hard. But his love is shown in the agonizing question, *When I come again, will God make me feel ashamed of you?* It is not basically their opinion of him that matters, but the quality of their Christian way of life.

One of the complaints against Paul was that he promised to visit Corinth and then, instead of coming himself, he sent a representative. In the sensitive atmosphere of Corinth this was variously interpreted as his fear to face them, his low opinion of them or his lack of real conviction that he could answer their charges. Letter-writing seemed to some to be a poor substitute for a visit and smacked of cowardice. So Paul makes much of this proposed *third visit*.

Vs 1-2 This will be my third visit to you. Remember the ancient Law: 'In the mouth of two or three witnesses shall every word be established.' My previous warning, given on my second visit, still stands and, though absent, I repeat it now as though I were present to those who had sinned before and to all the others, that my coming will not mean leniency.

Paul goes on to use the references to his power to lead him into a discussion of a very important theological issue. They respect power and he is trying to teach them the power of weakness. This is an incarnational theology. The life of a Christian should be orientated towards the life of Christ, in his weakness and in his power.

Vs 3-4 That will be the proof you seek that I speak by the power of Christ. The Christ you have to deal with is not a weak person outside you, but a tremendous power inside you. He was 'weak' enough to be crucified, yes, but he lives now by the power of God. We are weak as he was weak, but we are strong enough to deal with you for we share his life by the power of God.

Paul has had enough of justifying himself. He disliked the boasting, but they forced him to it. He realizes now that the Corinthians are doing harm to themselves by trying to set themselves up as judges of who is and who is not a true apostle. They should rather be looking carefully at their own lives to see if they measured up to the demands of the Christian life.

Vs 5–8 You should be looking at yourselves to make sure that you are really Christ's. It is yourselves that you should be testing. You ought to know by this time that Christ Jesus is in you, unless you are not real Christians at all. And when you have applied your test, I am confident that you will find that I myself am a genuine Christian. I pray God that you may make no mistake, not because I have any need of your approval, but because I earnestly want you to find the right answer, even if that should make me no real Christian. For we can make no progress against the truth; we can only work for it.

Paul is prepared to be rejected provided they have earnestly tested their own lives. This is his theory of an apostle; not one who lords it over them or demands that his authority be respected. An apostle is there to make them face the truth, and if he is the loser because of that he is quite prepared *to be weak*. Truth is what matters.

Vs 9–10 We are always quite happy to be weak if it means that you are strong. Our prayer for you is true Christian maturity. Hence the tone of this letter, so that when I do come I shall not be obliged to use with severity that power which the Lord has given me – though even that is not meant to break you down but to build you up.

Paul's concern is not to prove them wrong, *to break them down*, but to build them up. He uses here a technical term for building, and this is one of his most consistent themes. A building is being built for God, a temple.

And finally, a farewell, which like so much else in this letter has echoes of the worship of the church. *A handshake all round* misses what is probably a reference to a practice in the early church, 'the kiss of peace'. The letter ends with one of those rare trinitarian blessings. The three perfect gifts are listed; from *the Lord Jesus Christ, grace*; from *God, love*; from *the Holy Spirit*, a *fellowship* which only he can create.

Vs 11–14　Finally, then, my brothers, cheer up! Aim at perfection and accept my encouragement, agree with one another and live at peace. So shall the God of love and peace be ever with you.

A handshake all round, please! All the Christians here send greeting.

The grace of the Lord Jesus Christ, the love of God, and the fellowship that is ours in the Holy Spirit be with you all!

Also available in the Fontana Religious Series

What is Real in Christianity?
DAVID L. EDWARDS

The author strips away the legends from Jesus to show the man who is real, relevant and still fascinating. A clear, confident statement of Christian faith taking account of all criticisms.

Parents, Children and God
ANTHONY BULLEN

This book attempts to guide parents in their role as Christian educators. How they may answer their children's questions, how they may meet their children's needs from infancy to adolescence, how they may pray with their children, how they may talk to their children about sex: these and other topics are dealt with.

Ethics in a Permissive Society
WILLIAM BARCLAY

Professor Barclay approaches difficult and vexed questions with his usual humanity and clarity, asking what Christ himself would say or do in our world today.

Dialogue with Youth
AINSLIE MEARES

'This is a first-class general introduction to the world of young adults. . . . (It) is in general terms which convey a wealth of valuable insight . . . a quantity survey which helps to identify and map out a field of personal encounter in which few are competent, many are hesitant, all are involved.'

Church Times

Also available in the Fontana Religious Series

The Divine Pity
GERALD VANN

Undoubtedly Gerald Vann's masterpiece. Many people have insisted that this book should not merely be read, but re-read constantly, for it becomes more valuable the more it is pondered upon.

The Founder of Christianity
C. H. DODD

A portrait of Jesus by the front-ranking New Testament scholar. 'A first-rate and fascinating book . . . this book is a theological event.' *Times Literary Supplement*

Science and Christian Belief
C. A. COULSON

'Professor Coulson's book is one of the most profound studies of the relationship of science and religion that has yet been published.' *Times Literary Supplement*

Something Beautiful for God
MALCOLM MUGGERIDGE

'For me, Mother Teresa of Calcutta embodies Christian love in action. Her face shines with the love of Christ on which her whole life is centred. *Something Beautiful for God* is about her and the religious order she has instituted.'

Malcolm Muggeridge

Jesus Rediscovered
MALCOLM MUGGERIDGE

'. . . one of the most beautifully written, perverse, infuriating, enjoyable and moving books of the year.'

David L. Edwards, Church Times

Also available in the Fontana Religious Series

Something Beautiful for God
MALCOLM MUGGERIDGE

'For me, Mother Teresa of Calcutta embodies Christian love in action. Her face shines with the love of Christ on which her whole life is centred. *Something Beautiful for God* is about her and the religious order she has instituted.'

Malcolm Muggeridge

Instrument of Thy Peace
ALAN PATON

'Worthy of a permanent place on the short shelf of enduring classics of the life of the Spirit.'

Henry P. van Dusen, Union Theological Seminary

Sing A New Song
THE PSALMS IN TODAY'S ENGLISH VERSION

These religious poems are of many kinds: there are hymns of praise and worship of God; prayers for help, protection, and salvation; pleas for forgiveness; songs of thanksgiving for God's blessings; and petitions for the punishment of enemies. This translation of the *Psalms in Today's English Version* has the same freshness and clarity of language, the same accuracy of scholarship based on the very best originals available as *Good News for Modern Man* and *The New Testament in Today's English Version*.

The Gospel According to Peanuts
ROBERT L. SHORT

This book has made a lasting appeal to people of all denominations and none. It has been read and enjoyed by literally millions of people. A wonderfully imaginative experiment in Christian communication.

Also available in the Fontana Religious Series

The Prayer of the Universe
TEILHARD DE CHARDIN

A selection of Teilhard's most beautiful writings. This book will appeal to the thousands of readers who have read and re-read his best-sellers *Le Milieu Divin* and *Hymn of the Universe*.

To Me Personally
WILF WILKINSON

'When Wilf Wilkinson talks about the Bible, he makes it seem as though it has just been written, and not what some people think it is – 2,000 years out of date!'   *Roy Trevivian*

The Great Divorce
C. S. LEWIS

'It is all very witty, very entertaining, very readable, and Mr Lewis's fecundity of imagination is a thing to marvel at.'
Roger Lloyd, Time and Tide

The Difference in Being a Christian Today
JOHN A. T. ROBINSON

'Dr Robinson is addressing himself not to the rarefied world of *haute theologie* but to men of more modest academic pretensions or of none, which he does, nevertheless without talking down. . . . His is the theology of the people and for the people.'   *Clifford Longley, The Times*

Also available in the Fontana Religious Series

How Modern Should Theology Be?
HELMUT THIELICKE

'Thielicke touches on basic theological issues for today, but he does it with such a light hand, and with such graphic powers of illustration that I really cannot recall any other modern preacher who is so much *au fait* with modern theological questions.'
Ronald Gregor Smith

Strange Victory
GORDON W. IRESON

The Gospel, we are told, is Good News. What of? When we invite a man to become a Christian, what exactly are we offering to him, and asking him? These are some of the questions this book seeks to answer.

Companion to the Good News
JOSEPH RHYMER and ANTHONY BULLEN

More than 30 million people have bought *Good News for Modern Man* since it was first published. This 'Companion' has been written to help people understand the New Testament.

Apologia Pro Vita Sua
J. H. NEWMAN

A passionate defence of Cardinal Newman's own intellectual and spiritual integrity by a man who had been under continuous attack for many years.

Also available in the Fontana Religious Series

Double Zero
DAVID COLLYER

A fantastic story of a remarkable ministry; a story of courage, devotion and endurance to sustain and to succeed in an unorthodox ministry amongst Rockers in the city of Birmingham.

Don't Turn Me Off, Lord
CARL BURKE

'Short, pithy little essays' by the best-selling author of *God is for Real, Man.*

Where the Action Is
RITA SNOWDEN

Short sketches of interesting people from a wide variety of backgrounds: some famous and some who are not well-known. At the end of each story Rita Snowden sums up the theme in a short prayer.

The Parables of Peanuts
ROBERT L. SHORT

The Christian message is crystal clear and shows convincingly that Peanuts is essentially theological and deeply Christian.

Bible Stories
DAVID KOSSOFF

'To my mind there is no doubt that these stories make the Bible come alive. Mr Kossoff is a born story-teller. He has the gift of making the old stories new.'   *William Barclay*